ALL THE WAYS TO SAY I LOVE

"Compelling . . . a bleak vision redolent of classical tragedy."
—**Max McGuinness**, *Financial Times*

"LaBute's hour-long monologue is haunting . . . To say more is to spoil his perfect ending." —**David Finkle**, *The Huffington Post*

"A creeping primal darkness ensnares us in what appears to be an ordinary life."
—**Linda Winer**, *Newday*

"Beware of any mentions of *Reasons to be Happy* in Neil LaBute's dark new play . . . a wrenching solo monologue . . . unsettling to the haunting, heartrending end." —**Jennifer Farrar**, The Associated Press

"A densely plotted sonata . . . a portrait of a woman reckoning, without apology or deflection, with a decision that has defined her life."
—**Jason Fitzgerald**, *The Village Voice*

THE WAY WE GET BY

"It's sexy, it's starry . . . dangerously irresistible."
—**Ben Brantley**, *The New York Times*

"*The Way We Get By* has an unexpected sweetness, along with a twist."
—**Jennifer Farrar**, The Associated Press

"*The Way We Get By* feels like a refreshingly sunnier and more hopeful LaBute, with moments that feel suspiciously like giddy joy."
—**Sara Vilkomerson**, *Entertainment Weekly*

"Viscerally romantic, almost shockingly sensitive, even, dare we say it, sweet . . . LaBute . . . dares here to explore less obviously explosive territory. Yet, somehow, this daring feels deep." —**Linda Winer**, *Newsday*

THE MONEY SHOT

"A wickedly funny new comedy." —**Jennifer Farrar**, The Associated Press

"An acid-tongued showbiz satire." —**Scott Foundas**, *Variety*

"Fresh, joyously impolite . . . a good and mean little farce."
—**Linda Winer**, *Newsday*

"100 minutes of rapid-fire bursts of raucous laughter."
—**Michael Dale**, *BroadwayWorld*

"Packs a stunning amount of intelligence into 100 minutes of delectable idiocy."
—**Hayley Levitt**, *TheaterMania*

"Consistently entertaining . . . To his credit, LaBute does not aim for the obvious metaphor: in showbiz, everyone gets screwed. He is more concerned with amusing us." —**Brendan Lemon**, *Financial Times*

REASONS TO BE HAPPY

"Mr. LaBute is more relaxed as a playwright than he's ever been. He is clearly having a good time revisiting old friends . . . you're likely to feel the same way . . . the most winning romantic comedy of the summer, replete with love talk, LaBute-style, which isn't so far from hate talk . . ."
—**Ben Brantley**, *The New York Times*

"These working-class characters are in fine, foul-mouthed voice, thanks to the scribe's astonishing command of the sharp side of the mother tongue. But this time the women stand up for themselves and give as good as they get."
—**Marilyn Stasio**, *Variety*

"LaBute has a keen ear for conversational dialogue in all its profane, funny and inelegant glory." —**Joe Dziemianowicz**, *New York Daily News*

"LaBute . . . nails the bad faith, the grasping at straws, the defensive barbs that mark a tasty brawl." —**Elisabeth Vincentelli**, *New York Post*

"Intense, funny, and touching . . . In following up with the lives of his earlier characters, LaBute presents another compassionate examination of the ways people struggle to connect and try to find happiness."
—**Jennifer Farrar**, The Associated Press

"Terrifically entertaining." —**Philip Boroff**, *Bloomberg*

"A triumph . . . always electric with life. LaBute has a terrific way of demonstrating that even in their direst spoken punches . . . fighting lovers are hilarious. . . . completely convincing." —**David Finkle**, *Huffington Post*

REASONS TO BE PRETTY

"Mr. LaBute is writing some of the freshest and most illuminating American dialogue to be heard anywhere these days . . . *Reasons* flows with the compelling naturalness of overheard conversation. . . . It's never easy to say what you mean, or to know what you mean to begin with. With a delicacy that belies its crude vocabulary, *Reasons to be Pretty* celebrates the everyday heroism in the struggle to find out." —**Ben Brantley**, *The New York Times*

"There is no doubt that LaBute knows how to hold an audience. . . . LaBute proves just as interesting writing about human decency as when he is writing about the darker urgings of the human heart." —**Charles Spencer**, *Telegraph*

"Funny, daring, thought-provoking . . ." —**Sarah Hemming**, *Financial Times*

IN A DARK DARK HOUSE

"Refreshingly reminds us . . . that [LaBute's] talents go beyond glibly vicious storytelling and extend into thoughtful analyses of a world rotten with original sin." —**Ben Brantley**, *The New York Times*

"LaBute takes us to shadowy places we don't like to talk about, sometimes even to think about . . ." —**Erin McClam**, *Newsday*

WRECKS

"Superb and subversive . . . A masterly attempt to shed light on the ways in which we manufacture our own darkness. It offers us the kind of illumination that Tom Stoppard has called 'what's left of God's purpose when you take away God.'" —**John Lahr**, *The New Yorker*

"A tasty morsel of a play . . . The profound empathy that has always informed LaBute's work, even at its most stringent, is expressed more directly and urgently than ever here." —**Elysa Gardner**, *USA Today*

"*Wrecks* is bound to be identified by its shock value. But it must also be cherished for the moment-by-moment pleasure of its masterly portraiture. There is not an extraneous syllable in LaBute's enormously moving love story." —**Linda Winer**, *Newsday*

FAT PIG

"The most emotionally engaging and unsettling of Mr. LaBute's plays since *bash* . . . A serious step forward for a playwright who has always been most comfortable with judgmental distance." —**Ben Brantley**, *The New York Times*

"One of Neil LaBute's subtler efforts . . . Demonstrates a warmth and compassion for its characters missing in many of LaBute's previous works [and] balances black humor and social commentary in a . . . beautifully written, hilarious . . . dissection of how societal pressures affect relationships [that] is astute and up-to-the-minute relevant." —**Frank Scheck**, *New York Post*

THE DISTANCE FROM HERE

"LaBute gets inside the emptiness of American culture, the masquerade, and the evil of neglect. *The Distance From Here*, it seems to me, is a new title to be added to the short list of important contemporary plays." —**John Lahr**, *The New Yorker*

THE MERCY SEAT

"Though set in the cold, gray light of morning in a downtown loft with inescapable views of the vacuum left by the twin towers, *The Mercy Seat* really occurs in one of those feverish nights of the soul in which men and women lock in vicious sexual combat, as in Strindberg's *Dance of Death* and Edward Albee's *Who's Afraid of Virginia Woolf.*" —**Ben Brantley**, *The New York Times*

"A powerful drama . . . LaBute shows a true master's hand in gliding us amid the shoals and reefs of a mined relationship."

—**Donald Lyons**, *New York Post*

THE SHAPE OF THINGS

"LaBute . . . continues to probe the fascinating dark side of individualism . . . [His] great gift is to live in and to chronicle that murky area of not-knowing, which mankind spends much of its waking life denying." —**John Lahr**, *The New Yorker*

"LaBute is the first dramatist since David Mamet and Sam Shepard—since Edward Albee, actually—to mix sympathy and savagery, pathos and power."

—**Donald Lyons**, *New York Post*

"*Shape* . . . is LaBute's thesis on extreme feminine wiles, as well as a disquisition on how far an artist . . . can go in the name of art . . . Like a chiropractor of the soul, LaBute is looking for realignment, listening for a crack."

—**John Istel**, *Elle*

BASH

"The three stories in *bash* are correspondingly all, in different ways, about the power instinct, about the animalistic urge for control. In rendering these narratives, Mr. LaBute shows not only a merciless ear for contemporary speech but also a poet's sense of recurring, slyly graduated imagery . . . darkly engrossing."

—**Ben Brantley**, *The New York Times*

NEIL LABUTE is an award-winning playwright, filmmaker, and screenwriter. His plays include: *bash*, *The Shape of Things*, *The Distance From Here*, *The Mercy Seat*, *Fat Pig* (Olivier Award nominated for Best Comedy), *Some Girl(s)*, *Reasons to be Pretty* (Tony Award nominated for Best Play), *In a Forest, Dark and Deep*, a new adaptation of *Miss Julie*, and *Reasons to be Happy*. He is also the author of *Seconds of Pleasure*, a collection of short fiction, and a 2013 recipient of a Literature Award from the American Academy of Arts and Letters.

Neil LaBute's film and television work includes *In the Company of Men* (New York Critics' Circle Award for Best First Feature and the Filmmaker Trophy at the Sundance Film Festival), *Your Friends and Neighbors*, *Nurse Betty*, *Possession*, *The Shape of Things*, *Lakeview Terrace*, *Death at a Funeral*, *Some Velvet Morning*, *Ten x Ten*, *Dirty Weekend*, *Full Circle*, *Billy & Billie,* and *Van Helsing*.

ALL THE WAYS TO SAY I LOVE YOU

2 PLAYS + 1 STORY BY
NEIL LABUTE

OVERLOOK DUCKWORTH
NEW YORK · LONDON

This edition first published in the United States in 2016 by
Overlook Duckworth, Peter Mayer Publishers, Inc.

NEW YORK:
141 Wooster Street
New York, NY 10012
www.overlookpress.com
For bulk and special sales, please contact sales@overlookny.com,
or write to us at the address above.

LONDON:
30 Calvin Street
London E1 6NW
info@duckworth-publishers.co.uk
www.duckworth.co.uk
For bulk and special sales, please contact sales@duckworth-publishers.co.uk,
or write to us at the address above.

Cataloging-in-Publication Data is available from the Library of Congress

Book design and type formatting by Bernard Schleifer
Manufactured in the United States of America
ISBN 978-1-4683-1439-7 (US)
ISBN 978-0-7156-5191-9 (UK)
1 3 5 7 9 10 8 6 4 2

for judith and leigh

"i have everything, yet have nothing . . ."
—jean racine

CONTENTS

PREFACE

"For sale: baby shoes, never worn."

So goes the shortest of short stories attributed to Ernest Hemingway (though, like much of his life, there is contention as to whether this too is truth or fiction). I don't really care. I love that someone wrote it and I like to believe it was Hemingway. He sounds like the type of author who could write it—the man behind so much lean and muscular prose —and just the kind of person who would bet his fellow writers at Luchow's or the Algonquin that he could "write a complete novel in just six words" and then do so in such bravura fashion (fully collecting his earnings at the end of the wager as well, no doubt).

More importantly—and don't tell Mr. Hemingway this—I love the words and the story and how I feel every time I tell that tale or some-one tells it to me. I get the chills and the hairs on my arms stand at attention. Those six words are beautifully chosen and shaped and assembled into a complete cavalcade of woe. I feel them as a per-son, I love them as an artist and I agonize over them as a father.

As a writer, I envy the shit out of them and the person who created them (just in case it was Ms. Dorothy Parker instead of Mr. Heming-way, as previously reported).

That's actually one of the best feelings in the world when you're a writer. "Envy." Loving a piece of work by someone else so much that you wish that you had written it. It's not a bad thing. For me, to have written *Machinal* instead of Sophie Treadwell or *All My Sons* instead of Arthur Miller or *Disgrace* instead of J.M. Coetzee or *The Secret History* instead of Donna Tartt would be a wonderful thing and I envy each and every word that those authors wrote instead of me. In a good way. In a healthy way that says "thank you for being so damn great and for setting the bar so damn high and for taking me to places with your writing that I still need to go in my own." It's nice to have heroes—in both your real and your literary life—and I don't see anything wrong with a little healthy competition.

If you can impress me in just six words, even better.

I have written at some length about how much I value the short literary form in playwriting but I could just as easily go on about my love of the short story. I recently read through a volume of Shirley Jackson's best work and was taken aback at how gorgeous and bone-chilling her stories could be. Beautiful words, assembled into little collages of pain and regret. Run out and grab a collection if you can, if you love reading or writing or simply get off on hearing about misfortune in regard to other people. You will be thankful that the collective fates of her protagonists have not fallen on your slender shoulders, believe you me (and I don't mean just the particularly gruesome one that befalls poor Mrs. Hutchinson in "The Lottery," probably the most well-known of Ms. Jackson's work).

The volume that you now have in front of you is a strange little beast. It contains two short plays and the short story that inspired those two dramatic works. My editor and I thought that by bringing these three literary forms together (prose, monologue, and playlet), one might get a clearer picture of their individual and collective creation and get some small glimpse into how an idea can grow and shift and turn back on itself as it is birthed by a writer.

"With Hair of Hand-Spun Gold" was a commissioned work for a collection of new fairy tales; I got involved thanks to the wonderful writer Kate Bernheimer and my offering to *My Mother She Killed Me, My Father He Ate Me* (great title) was a modern re-telling of "Rumplestiltskin." Ever the outsider, I told the story from the perspective of the troublesome Mr. Rumplestiltskin and in a first-person form. To my knowledge it's never been performed as a monologue but it certainly could be. In it, a young man talks about his relationship with a teacher and the kinds of joy and misery that come from this cursed and calculated union. By the time I decided to write a one-woman show loosely based on the myth of Phaedra, I doubled back and used the same ideas that had led me to my fairy tale, but this time from the perspective of the teacher in question.

All The Ways To Say I Love You is a full-on monologue that gives us the story of an older woman and a younger man completely from the side of the woman. She recounts their history (and the history of her life with her husband) as she finishes up her day at high school. She is also a counselor to these students and we see her putting away their files and writing notes to herself while explaining to us how she began and ended an illicit affair with a young man and to what purpose (and that purpose may be even darker than you think).

Because there's always a purpose to things.

As much as we try to tell ourselves "this just happened" or "I didn't mean anything by that" the truth is that this is hardly ever the case. Things tend to happen for a reason, some driven by our own needs (or wants) and sometimes by the needs (or wants) of others. That is certainly the case in *All The Ways To Say I Love You* and hearing a seemingly well-adjusted and caring woman tell us in quiet and rational terms how she could push the envelope of "love" to such extremes is a sobering journey and a lesson well worth learning.

I love writing in the monologue form and it was a pleasure to lose myself in the character of "Mrs. Johnson." To listen to her voice as she told her story, to give words to her desires and to help fuel her calculations until she had seen her plans through to the bitter end. It was fun and a kick but I'm glad it was all on paper and nobody actually got hurt in the process.

To get a chance to work with the theater company MCC on our 10th full-length play is such an amazing event—that it is this play shows how deep their commitment to new work is. I want to thank the collective artistic team there—Bernard Telsey, Will Cantler and Robert Lupone—along with their great literary manager, Stephen Willems, for taking many chances on me and my work and for always being honest about my writing. It's never easy to tell someone you know and like that their work isn't good enough or not good enough yet and these folks have been kind and strong enough to do just that to me many times over. Their collective honesty has made me a better writer.

The fact that the director Leigh Silverman and the actress Judith Light are bringing *All The Ways To Say I Love You* to life on stage speaks to how absolutely lucky and blessed I have been as a writer for the theater. Two brilliant women combining to create the world of "Mrs. Johnson." It doesn't get much better than that.

And then I wrote *All My White Sins Forgiven* because I needed to hear from "Eric" as well. "Eric" is the husband of "Mrs. Johnson" and someone, I felt, who needed a voice in this triangle of love and lust. To hear his words, I decided on a short play—a two-hander—that would give us a bit of Eric's world-view and a sense of the man that perhaps even his own wife doesn't know. Philip Levine (a fellow Detroiter) supplied me with the provocative title and the rest just spilled out of me—I love writing for and about men and can do it all day long. The weird camaraderies, the silly, almost sexual banter between friends and the petty rivalries. It's great stuff. It's always a huge compliment to be told "you write well for women" and I'm glad that's part of what I can do but finding the jungle rhythms in the banter of boys is one of my favorite things ever.

And we do remain boys. Most of our lives.

J.M. Barrie really got it right: if we could, most of us would stay boys for the rest of our days. This is both a good and bad thing. I've stayed youthful in my life and my writing and it's helped me a great deal as an author. As a person around me—family member, loved one, etc.—it's probably been filled with good days and bad years and endless frustrations. I'm sorry for that (and a million and one other things) but I've bumbled along about as well as I could for someone who has always been afraid and has often been abused and tried to be a man but more than occasionally reverted to being a child. Worse than baby shoes never worn, there have been several adult pairs of shoes that I have never adequately worn (not yet, anyway) and I am sorry for that as well.

I did try and I'll keep on trying. I promise.

The best thing I can do is write. That's what I've learned along the way. Be it six words or six thousand, I am a writer. It's is my gift and my curse. It is who I am and the best of what I can be.

I believe the words inside this book represent me well. I trust that you too will find it so.

Neil LaBute
August 2016

ALL THE WAYS TO SAY I LOVE YOU

All The Ways To Say I Love You had its world premiere at the Lucille Lortel Theatre (MCC) in New York City in September 2016.
It was directed by Leigh Silverman.

MRS. JOHNSON   Judith Light

Silence. Darkness.

A chair. Center stage. That is all.

After a moment, a woman enters and sits. Several files in one hand that go to her lap when she is settled in the chair.

She sits quietly for a moment, listening to the sound of an old classic playing somewhere. One of the greats, like Peggy Lee or Nina Simone.

Someone like that.

As this fades away, she begins to speak:

MRS. JOHNSON   . . . "how much?" she wonders. (*Beat.*) A girl in my class. "What is the weight of a lie?" And at first, I think perhaps I haven't heard her correctly. I say "What?" and I ask her to repeat what she's said . . . but I didn't mishear her . . . I have heard her correctly. "How much does a lie weigh?" She wants to know . . . *but* in ounces . . . or pounds . . . or however you would do it. Weigh it out. You see, I had once made reference to the weight of a "soul" . . . which has been argued over by scholars and poets and priests for years . . . and I had mentioned it to her in passing, and so here she is now, asking the same thing about a "lie." How much it might weigh. The *weight* of it. Her father is a butcher and *that's* what she wants to know . . . the weight of a lie in practical terms . . . and for once . . . I don't have an answer. I pride myself on answers. It's the sign of a good teacher, or that's what I've been taught, anyway . . . a million years ago. Not even the right one, that isn't even important, but to offer up *an* answer. That's what our job is. As instructors. Guides. Teachers. To put forth a possibility, one idea or an assumption or . . . a truth, even, if such a thing really exists out there—the *truth*—*that* is what we do. We are asked things every day . . . over and over . . . and each time we must take the time to give an answer back. If it's right, then that's a wonderful thing . . . and if it's wrong, then together we will discover that and work it out as a team, in groups of two or three or *ten*—as an entire classroom, even—and we will find out what is right and what is wrong. But that first one . . . that *initial* answer . . . that's for me to say. To teach. To lead. To be an example. I've done it for thirty years now, or something very close to that . . . and I love it. It's what I was meant to do with my life and I think I still do it with a kind of passion and energy and . . . well, with a kind of *zest*, even . . . that speaks for itself. And yet . . . I had nothing for this girl who asked me about lies and their weight and, I mean, rationally I think "Well, it's probably subjective, in some way . . . each one must weigh a certain amount based on this and this or that . . ." but now I wonder if that is true. I wonder. (*Beat.*) It's been years since whomever posed that question to me . . . but I've thought about it many times since then, and the answer . . . if there is a correct one out there in the universe somewhere . . . it has eluded me . . . no matter how much I puzzle over it or *Google* it or try to track it down . . . (*Beat.*) "What is the weight of a lie . . .?"

She puts one folder aside and glances at another one. She indicates the pages within and then begins to speak:

But this is not about that . . . this is about *this* . . . and so that's
what we'll do . . . we will talk about this and not that . . . not about
lies and how much they may or may not weigh. And who knows?
The truth . . . in the end, might surprise us all . . . even me. (*Beat.*)
Yes, even *me*.

She rustles through a few more pages and then turns to us. Begins to
tell her story:

. . . he was a good-looking boy but I don't think that's why he
was the one I chose. I mean, it didn't hurt anything, obviously,
but . . . that was not the *reason* that I picked him . . . not just that,
anyway. I'm not really a "looks" person . . . so . . . no. (*Beat.*) He
walked into my office one afternoon . . . this was a Thursday,
I think . . . might've been on a Friday, I usually did a half-day on
Fridays but that winter semester I remember I was doing a few
longer hours end of the week so I could build up my holidays . . .
we were planning on taking a few extra days over the spring
break and this was making that possible . . . Eric and I, that's what
we'd planned for our vacation. When you're a teacher, it becomes
important to just go with the flow . . . take your days off when
everybody else does and to embrace the summertime because
very quickly it's August again and there you go, back to the classroom and starting over on whatever it is that your specialty is. I do
English. Well, English and Drama, but what that means is I pick a
play each year for the "thespians" to perform—in the Fall—and
help out with the Spring Musical. Nothing musical on my part . . .
I can barely *whistle* a note . . . but the dramatic or comedic bits.
The *acting*. I would oversee those parts and then also all the
settings, too . . . get my students involved in building the sets and
that sort of thing . . . make-up and ticket sales, all the other as-

pects of production when the time came. That's what I would do. (*Beat.*) He came to my office when I was in the process of picking the play for the coming year, in fact—I was also a counselor for grade twelve as well—and he was assigned to me after his usual counselor was out on her maternity leave . . . *so* . . . that's how we ended up together, on that Thursday. Or Friday. Whichever it was. (*Beat.*) He had actually been a student of mine during his first year at school . . . my school, I mean. Jefferson High. 9th grade . . . but I don't think he remembered it. We were doing *Lord of the Flies* and most kids can recall the year they read that, it's one of those books that usually . . . well . . . it has the ability to leave some kind of mark on everybody who reads it . . . especially the boys, but Tommy was out a lot that year . . . I think his mom was getting a divorce—*another* one . . . from the sound of the gossip around school . . . or the teacher's lounge, anyway . . . and that's never easy for a kid . . . no matter what age you are or how many times you go through it . . . it's just never easy. I know that part for a fact. (*Beat.*) And I think Tommy had gone through it a *lot* . . . a couple times already. Once or twice, at least. That's what it said in his file, anyway, but that information is not always accurate and it's not something you can just blurt right out and ask a student, first time you meet 'em. Or *counsel* them, anyway. He dropped plenty of hints, of course, small things . . . stuff that you wouldn't actually be able to call him on if you needed to . . . things about his step-father and how much he hated the guy and that sort of thing . . . it felt like he was covering for his mom and he probably was. Kids do that. Cover. No matter what you do to them, no matter how horrible you act . . . kids love their moms . . . that is just a fact. (*Beat.*) Anyhow, Tommy's mother had made yet another mistake in life and love and it was her son who was trying to make it all better—and I see that behavior every day of the week in this job, and I mean *every* damn day . . . (*Beat.*) I'm not someone who swears a lot, but occasionally this job gets to you . . . (*Beat.*) And that is an understatement. (*Beat.*) It ALWAYS gets to you . . . just sometimes more than others.

She stops at this, unsure whether to go on or not.

His grades weren't terrible, actually. I mean . . . yes, not great . . . but for a second-year Senior who had been to the office practically every day of his life and a person who had no assistance at home whatsoever and probably also had some kind of behavior disorder—he wasn't bi-polar or ADHD, or anything like that, but he was definitely one of those people who could change the temperature in a classroom just by staring out the window or asking a question or, you know, making a face . . . a face like . . . you know . . . like *this*. (*She attempts to re-create "the face."*) That face that says "Man, this sucks . . ." (*Beat.*) I mentioned Eric a minute ago, didn't I? Said his name, at least, without saying who he is or . . . sorry! I do that on occasion, not that I mean to, or . . . I'm not scattered, I'm definitely not that—I've received two different citations for my teaching over the years, and one of them was *city-wide*—but, yes, I can be a little forgetful sometimes. Or get off on a tangent . . . like I am right now. Sorry! (*Beat.*) "Eric." My husband. (*Beat.*) He's of *mixed-race* . . . not that this is how I see him or think of him or whatnot . . . I don't . . . not firstly, anyhow, but it's something that he's very . . . what's the right way to . . . he takes a certain *pride* in it. I think he does . . . maybe now more than he did when I first met him. Eric is quick to point it out and wears it around a bit. Not, like, in your face, I don't mean that, but since the last few elections . . . there is a kind of . . . well, you know what I'm saying. (*Beat.*) He certainly used it along the way . . . during college and admission to law school, with some loans or . . . not even that . . . not for loans but the other ones, the what-do-you-call-ems? Umm . . . the free ones . . .? (*Considering.*) Grants. He received quite a few grants in his time for government funds . . . as a result of his being "mixed" or a person of color. God . . . it all changes so quickly and so often . . . what we can call a person who's . . . *Negro* was the one we used at first—right or wrong, it was widely accepted—then "black" and then every-thing had to be "African-American" for a long time, and now we're back to "black" again. People who are that—black, I mean—they use a number of other phrases for themselves as well, including the "N" word, all the time . . . over and over, and as they do, they kind of look at you as they do it, almost sort of defiantly . . . to see if we're going to say anything. I say "we" meaning white people, I suppose, but it's anyone who's not black that I really mean. They do it in restaurants or on the train . . . when they see each other as a greeting or when they start laughing and telling a story about someone, or when they get mad as well . . . apparently it's totally fine if they do it . . . and I mean in *any* context. *Ever.* But you can't point that out . . . because it will not end well. That is a sure-fire way for voices to be raised and a lot of screaming and indignation, that kind of thing . . . every time. I've seen it so many times over the years in our lounge—teachers getting into it with each other, or with substitutes—it's just not worth it. No. And it's happened to me as well, obviously. Married to Eric. Even with him . . . "you don't get it, you just do not get it. You can't possibly understand." That's an argument I just . . . well, I steer clear of because it is impossible to win. Not that I need to . . . I'm not that person . . . someone who has to win arguments and I rarely get into situations like that . . . where I raise my voice and get carried away, but it is just . . . well, it's nice to know you at least have a *chance* to be heard . . . and if I did find myself in a place like that, in an argument, and someone would just sit and calmly listen to what I have to say . . . it would be this: Throw it out. Get rid of it entirely. It has done nothing but harm, created pain and hardship and ill will from the day it was first uttered . . . I mean, we were talking earlier about the weight of things. Can you even imagine what the weight of that one might be? That word? So we end it, forever— we get rid of it. That "N" word . . . "nigger" . . . we outlaw it, and execute it, and we bury it in an unmarked grave outside of town. (*Laughs.*) God! Listen to me! I'll stop now. (*Beat.*) So . . . anyway . . . back to Eric . . . my husband. A lawyer. A good man and someone I love . . . and I have for a long, long time. Since grad school, really . . . which is . . . well, I'll never tell! (*Grins.*) Just know it was a while ago now . . .

She thinks about this for a moment and she smiles at the thought of it. Her eyes glisten with tears as well, but mostly she smiles.

But I was—see? I do get off-topic! Twice! But this is about "Tommy" and me. What happened between the two of us. (*Beat.*) He'd come to me on that Thursday . . . or Friday . . . I *honestly* don't remember which now . . . and he was interested in whether he might still get in to some college if he could pull some of his grades up . . . maybe do well on the SAT. A normal question for a Senior . . . even one like Tommy. A second-year Senior who lived in a lousy home with a mother who thought of no one but herself and did absolutely nothing to help her child. Well . . . one of five children, actually. At least four of whom had different dads—and I am not judging her, I'm honestly not—I mean, not *too* much . . . but those were the odds against him . . . when he came in to see me. (*Beat.*) That was what I was dealing with when he sat down in my office with me. Tommy.

She shuffles a few papers, looking through a file for something that she wants to read out loud.

Nothing happened between us that day. Not on that first day, there in my school office. I mean, there was . . . I could feel a *certain* . . . he was close to me, when he pulled his chair over so we could look through some of the catalogs on my desk . . . there were a few points where his leg would brush up against mine and he would hold it . . . hold himself up against me like that . . . not in any sort of obvious way, I don't mean that, but so that we could both . . . you know . . . register it. That we were touching. His leg up against mine . . . and I didn't pull back from it either. (*Beat.*) I fully acknowledge that right now—I might not have on that day, I might've said you were crazy or seeing things or imagining what-ever . . . but I can see it all fairly clearly now and yes . . . I knew that he was pushing me in those first moments, sort of just gently pushing me to see what was possible . . . and what wasn't. (*Beat.*) Obviously, contact with my leg was "possible." (*Beat.*) And it went on from there. For a long time after that. (*Beat.*) It's difficult to say what began it . . . how I let it go as far as it went, but I mean, how do most affairs begin in the first place? Hmmmmm? Because something is *missing* in the first place . . . and obviously, that was the case with Eric and me as well. (*Beat.*) Eric is a kind man . . . he's decent and gentle . . . I think when we talk he hears me and responds, doesn't speak down to me in that way that successful people can do sometimes . . . but he was not a great lover. He was not someone who took your breath away in the bedroom and

that's just . . . that is simply a fact. A fact of life, my life with him
. . . and our life as a couple. I think that I bring him pleasure—I know
I can make him orgasm, or *"cum"* or however you want to say it
. . . and the evidence of that with men is . . . you know . . . much,
much clearer with a man than the other way around. So, slowly,
along the way, I became one of those people. Someone who lied
in bed. Said it was "good" . . . that I was *satisfied*, but that was
not the truth. To this day . . . that is not the truth. With Eric. (*Beat.*)
But I love him. I do. I think I've proved that now . . . along the way,
with all that's happened, but . . . it's always nice to know. To hear
it. So, yes: I love my husband. (*Beat.*) We've gone through so
much together . . . over the years and the struggling to have children. It's not easy. Not for a man and certainly not for a "man of
color." It speaks to something, a deep rooted sense of self and,
and . . . I'm not even sure what . . . but something that haunted
Eric for a long time afterward. Because of this . . . our less than
successful sex life and the difficulty we were having trying to
conceive a child—it was not impossible, our doctor was quick to
stress . . . (*Imitates his voice.*) *It is not out of the realm of possibility,
but, however . . .* and I would listen and nod and hope and Eric
would walk out of the room . . . so, it was not out of the realm of
possibility but it was very unlikely and that was that and I was now
getting older and so it seemed that this was going to pass us by,
that part of a life together . . . we would not grow old together as
parents . . . one of the few things Eric really wanted in life. One of
the very few. And somehow . . . it came to feel as if this was my
problem. That it was my fault . . . no matter what tests said . . .
no matter what his sperm count was . . . no matter how often we

would have passionate and empty debates about adoption—an idea that Eric just couldn't stomach, the idea of us raising some other man's child—so there it was. This void between us. (*Beat.*) And yet I loved him and still do and so many other parts of our life together were and continue to be full and rich and honestly perfect. Even with this dark patch that hovered over us . . . each night as we'd linger in the living room just a bit longer before going upstairs to bed . . . or each time we tried to make love or make a child . . . despite *all* that we made a good and handsome couple and I love him and I think he feels the same about me . . . (*Beat.*) God, I suppose you'd have to ask him if that's true or not, but I think so. I really do think that's the truth. (*Beat.*) That my husband loves me . . .

She stops for a moment, takes a sip from a glass nearby. Waits. Begins again:

The sexual . . . I guess you'd call it just "sex" . . . but . . . the "sex" with Tommy was quite different. It was unlike anything I'd ever had before in my life . . . not that I really want to go into that now, with any sort of detail, but . . . most of you know what I mean when I say . . . wow. That's such a childish word to use, for an adult like myself, but . . . sometimes it's the only thing that will do. The things we did . . . the kind of just . . . *release* . . . that I experienced with that young man . . . I can't feel bad about it . . . everyone should have that chance . . . at some point in their lives . . . to know what that can feel like. Just . . . yeah. Yes. Wow. (*Beat.*) For a young person . . . a boy almost . . . the things he would do, think up to do . . . were kind of shocking. Maybe they just have more stamina or . . . or they're just naughtier today . . . that might be it, with what's out there on television and on the Internet and at the movies . . .

there are a lot more images and filmclips a person could see or
. . . you know . . . wonder about . . . want to try out on another
person . . . I'm not sure how he knew to do what he did to me . . .
but he did it . . . and it was quite breathtaking . . . no matter what
the cost was. In the end. (*Beat.*) For a time we did things to each
other—things I really can't even imagine *suggesting* to Eric . . .
let alone doing . . . and yet I did all of them with this boy . . . *so*
eagerly . . . and with *such* abandon . . . that I am not ashamed.
Even now. I'm not at all ashamed and even the thought of some
of those moments can make me shudder inside with a kind of real
. . . *ecstasy* . . . a sort of longing and an absolute sense of desire
for him—right up to this very day. I mean, my God . . . this young
man who brings me such great pleasure and I do the same for
him. Because I did, oh my God, did I ever . . . do things to him and
make him scream and . . . and . . . well . . . you know. Yes. I did
that. All that. Just . . . unforgettable. (*Beat.*) And to say these
things out loud, to tell anyone I know about this . . . I would be a
pariah. Hissed at. While a man, any man doing the same thing?
A slap on the back and a knowing wink . . . the disparity between
the sexes, when it comes to sex, is astonishing. Even now. Even
today . . . disgusting. But that's not . . . here I am, once again. Off
topic. Forgive me. (*Beat.*) I *know* that I misled him . . . not just in the
usual sense of the older person in the situation . . . of a teacher
misleading a student . . . I did all of that, too, of course, but I went even
further . . . so much further than even that . . . (*Smiles.*) I shouldn't
smile. It's not at all appropriate and it's not because I'm happy or
proud or, or . . . but it's not shame, I know that much. It's not one
of those smiles you do when you're in a moment of panic or caught
out . . . it's not that, either. It's just . . . there was a moment there
where I had it all. My life with Eric. A job that I liked and was re-

spected for and then . . . for a few short months . . . I had Tommy as well. Tommy. Doing things to me . . . with his mouth and his . . . you know what I mean . . . things that I had never, *ever* felt in my entire life. And it was good. It was so, so good. (*Beat.*) . . . it couldn't last and it didn't but while it did . . . I was in a kind of Heaven that I have never been a part of before or since . . . (*Beat.*) But yes, I did lie to him about things to have it all my way. I did do that . . . and yet, even now, with what's going on . . . I don't think that I would've done it any other way. I really, really don't. (*Beat.*) Eric was easy enough. That took very little work, to find time after school or on weekends to get away, to meet up with Tommy, that was simple, really. We were so deep into our marriage at that point . . . so much a couple but so consumed by our own private things . . . a little fib here or two words there implying a meeting or a luncheon or a movie . . . and I was free to do as I liked. That was the easy part. Eric. (*Beat.*) But Tommy—he was a different challenge all-together. Making him stay hungry for me . . . wanting more of what he knew he shouldn't ever even be having . . . to keep that going was what took so much time . . . but it was just so . . . perfect. For a few months there. Honestly . . . no matter what it's like for you to hear . . . it's more important for me to say it clearly and truthfully out loud because it's honestly how I feel . . . I *loved* it! Every second of every day when that boy was fucking me . . . I LOVED it!!

She stops for a moment, overcome by the thought of what has passed between the two of them. After a beat, she continues:

I did, I *loved* it and because of that, the way it made me feel when I was with him . . . *Tommy* . . . it began to overtake me. Made me willing to do *any*thing . . . to take risks . . . risks that no one should ever take—certainly not a teacher of children, a *married* teacher of children with several service awards under her belt and a respected place in the community . . . no . . . there is no reason at all to be doing what I was doing and yet there I was . . . doing it . . . *things* . . . sneaking around town, meeting up like teenagers in the back of my car and . . . and . . . and . . . *no.* You know what? That is not at all true. It isn't. We met up, Tommy and I, through all of those months . . . in plain sight. We did. Right out there under everybody's nose . . . and why is that? Do you know *why* we were able to do it that way? Hmmm? Do you? You're looking at it. The reason. "Me." People saw us together, many times—school and in the parking lot . . . at a bookstore one time and at *lunch* even . . . *two* towns over—and not once did anyone bat an eye at us, not one single suspicious eyelash . . . because of *me* . . . how people saw *me* . . . felt about *me.* My hair. My clothes. My life. (*Imitating someone.*) "*Them*? No way! I mean, *no* way could there be anything going on between those two. It's just *not* possible!" That was the image I projected as a person . . . a woman . . . a sexual being. (*Beat.*) I was married to Eric and that was that . . . and all that could ever be. *That* was who I am. (*Beat.*) And that *very* thing allowed Tommy and me to carry on . . . the way we did . . . in public . . . out in the open . . . in broad daylight. I mean, what young man in his right mind would *ever* want an older woman, an older *married* woman like me? Hmmmm? WHO? (*Smiles.*) Who indeed?

Another sip. She carefully replaces the glass and takes a beat again before she continues:

The day that I told Eric the news was . . . well, it was complicated. To say the least! It was complicated. But what took over, the second that I said something, alluded to it . . . was such joy.

Such happiness. For him and me. Of the many ways to say
"I love you" . . . a child may be the most perfect of them all . . .
(*Beat.*) It was, well . . . it was how I always imagined it was going
to be, when it finally happened . . . and it did happen. Finally.
In all of those years . . . all those demeaning and dehumanizing
tests that he and I went through—egg counts and the blood
draws and the sperm samples—through all of that, I never gave
up hope for it to happen. I never gave up on us. And I know he
did, know it for a fact—Eric did—but that's alright, I can understand it and accept it . . . as a man, as a "man of color" (as he
will always point out in times like those) . . . it's different for him.
I know it and I embrace it. He gave up. He decided it would never
happen for us and I think—I don't know for sure, I honestly do
not—but I believe that he may have even been . . . there was a
year or so there in our marriage where I wouldn't have been
surprised to learn that he was with another woman, or more than
one . . . an affair, a mistake, an escort . . . none of it would've
shocked me. He was taking more and more work out of town,
or work that took him out of town—"business trips," as they love
to call them—and I could feel something in the air. That . . .
good between us . . . slowly evaporating . . . and I resolved to
fix it. To mend that. To find a way out of a bad situation. (*Beat.*)
And I did. (*Beat.*) I don't want to mislead you . . . Eric and
I continued to make love when time allowed, or when it felt like
we should—husbands and wives know those moments, people
in most relationships do . . . but man and wife, they are so so
conscious of that moment . . . when they *should* be making love.
Even if it's the most perfunctory experience, we know when we
need to touch our partners and make them feel as if we are still
interested and involved . . . it just comes with the territory. And so

Eric and I would do that—once a week, sometimes more, usually less—moments of touching or intercourse, something simple and oral. Whatever it took. To keep up the appearance of lust because that's what it was, really . . . the *appearance* of it. I mean, there was certainly still love there . . . to this day . . . I *love* him, and I would do anything to keep us together. Anything, and I have done that . . . so much . . . gone so far . . . and I would do it all again, every step I've taken . . . every ill that I've committed . . . whatever you or anyone else would call illegal or unnatural or just plain . . . *wrong*, I'd do a thousand times over. To have what I have in my life today. (*Beat.*) I don't feel I'm alone in that . . . feeling that way, about my life . . . most people I know have strung together so many little crimes, dozens and dozens of tiny deceits . . . to live in the place that they do, with the person that they live with; and perhaps I'm kidding myself, trying to feel better about what I did and helping myself to sleep at night . . . but I don't think so . . . I think *this* is "life" . . . what I've done, right here. You act or you don't act. You do something or you don't. There is only today. There is only tomorrow. Yesterday is just a puff of smoke . . . without recourse, without punishment or remorse . . . am I crazy to think that? (*Beat.*) Don't answer me . . . I don't think I really wanna know the truth about that one. Not about that . . .

She adjusts a lamp on the table. Keeping the glare out of her face. She is about to speak, stops, then starts again:

The months after that . . . after we found out that we were about to become parents for the first time, those were the trickiest. I had to be so careful . . . so predatory . . . had to play things so precisely, always on the edge of being found out . . . that it was exhausting for me. As I look back on it now . . . I'm amazed that

I could pull it off . . . how it was even possible . . . but I did it. I absolutely did. (*Beat.*) Without raising his suspicion, I had to begin to break things off with Tommy and also help him move on with his life—I'm sure this has sounded very one-sided, as if it was only about me—my pleasure . . . my desire for a child—but that's absolutely not true. It just isn't. I really did want to help Tommy . . . from that first day he walked into my office, I wanted to help him out of the situation he was in and that is what I did. Perhaps with . . . a bit more urgency than I would've with another student . . . that's probably very true . . . but I just want to make that point because it's important to me, that you understand that . . . I was *helping* Tommy during all this and not just *using* him. No matter what you or anybody else might say about it . . . I honestly believed in him and, in my own way . . . I was saving him. I know that word is . . . but, yes, I was. I was "saving" him. By this time Tommy and I were . . . well . . . basically over. We were . . . I mean . . . I would still meet him occasionally, not for sex, not for that anymore, but just to be with him and try to help him understand that I needed to stay where I was—in my marriage, with my husband —as much as I liked being with him, and I did, I've told you as much, I did enjoy it, but there was just no way . . . obviously no way on this earth that what we were doing was going to ever have a life of its own . . . I mean . . . come on, that had to be obvious, even to him. This was not going to be some kind of a fairy tale romance or . . . we were not about to run away together and hope for the best . . . love conquers all . . . I mean, *please* . . . I teach it but I don't believe in it: drama. Not that kind of "drama," anyway. I'm too old for that . . . even then I was, and that was years ago . . . I wasn't about to go on the run with this boy and start over in another town, with our child on the way—that was just NOT gonna happen.

No . . . not ever. I suppose . . . I mean, yes, it's possible that in
Tommy's heart . . . or head . . . it may've felt like there was something that had a chance of happening . . . people can talk themselves into almost anything, they really can . . . so I'm not sure
what Tommy might have imagined that we actually had going on
. . . what *his* perfect world for us may've been. But for me, he was
a means to an end. A beautiful, sweet means, to be sure . . . but
yes, that's what he was to me. A way to keep the life I had with
Eric alive and well . . . and at the same time, I was absolutely
ready to help Tommy out as well. And I did. (*Beat.*) That boy went
to college because of *me* . . . that young man now has a job in IT
because of *me* . . . the time that I took helping him and pushing
him to do better . . . Tommy is what he is because of me and that
is not bragging or exaggerating or anything of the sort. That is the
simple and undeniable truth of the matter. What chance does a
boy like that have in this world without a person like me helping
him? (*Beat.*) He is what he is now because of *me*, and I don't
mean that in a sort of racial way, either . . . I am not that person,
a person who'd do that or say it or even imply it . . . *look* at me.
The work I do, the life I lead. It has not always been easy being
married to Eric. My father, friends of the family . . . couples who
pass us on the streets sometimes . . . *yes*, we have made
progress as a people and as a country, but believe me, live this
way and you'll see that I am telling you the truth . . . we have a
LONG way to go. A VERY long way. I'm not talking about the
streets of New York City and I don't mean a new generation of
students and young people who have a wonderful and healthier
sense of what *love* and *family* can be . . . I am talking about an
America that simply does not believe in equality and that's highly
suspect of a black man and a white woman who publicly kiss and

say "I love you." *Yes*, even today. Believe me . . . there are still many folks out there who are more than happy to see those marriages fail and whisper behind the backs of the mixed boys and girls of those unholy unions—just ask Eric, my husband. (*Beat.*) Eric will be VERY happy to discuss this topic with you . . . believe me. My husband is a smiler and a hand-shaker but inside . . . in his innermost heart of hearts . . . he trusts *no* one. Finds *every* gesture suspect. Believes *all* white men are out to get him, and he's probably right. In some way. In some simple, awful way . . . it's true. Eric knows it . . . I know it . . . the world knows it . . . and that is the weight that any man of color carries around on his shoulders today. Still *today*. (*Beat.*) There were a few close calls, one in particular that was . . . well, it probably brought things to where they are today, now that I think back on it . . . it certainly didn't help anything . . . I can tell you that much! It didn't help things at all . . . (*Beat.*) Eric and I were walking in the mall . . . this was on a weekend, I remember it like it was yesterday. I was only probably five months in at this time, just starting to show now and . . . you know . . . I was *glowing* at this point. Everybody said so. It was months since I'd last seen or been around Tommy —summer was on us and we were enjoying a few days of quiet time, Eric and I. School was done, Tommy had graduated and was now poised to begin college at a school downstate . . . many hundreds of miles away . . . he had come by my office one afternoon, very late in the semester, and he just popped his head in through the door, as he was known to do—and he pledged his love to me. Said that he understood our "situation" and that he'd take it like a "man" but that he's always gonna "love" me. Just like that. Said "I love you . . . and I'm always gonna." And I was . . . God, some part of me wanted to just run over to him . . . throw my arms around him and . . . and . . . but the rest of me, the very practical part of me . . . hoped that no one in the office over from mine had heard him . . . that is what I was thinking as he's standing there, smiling at me . . . and I was smiling back. Frozen. Terrified now . . . that everything I'd done . . . *so* carefully . . . might backfire . . . right at the very last moment . . . (*Beat.*) But it didn't . . . it did not . . . (*Beat.*) Anyhow! The mall! Eric and I were walking down past Penney's, on our way out to the car, his arm around me—I hadn't seen him this happy about anything, the way he was about this baby in so long . . . for . . . so many years . . . and suddenly . . . I hear a voice from behind me. "Mrs. Johnson?" And we both turn, Eric and I . . . and there is Tommy, holding hands with some girl whom I vaguely recognize as a Freshman or a Sophomore or something from our school, with this look in his eyes. Smiling at me. At both of us. Me and Eric. I instinctively cover myself with the shopping bags in my hands as I do my best to meet his eye, quickly introducing him as one of my students as we share some small talk . . . Tommy's already moved down to school but just up for a cousin's birthday and seeing friends, going to take a load of his things down to his dorm after that—Eric stands there and talks to the boy, smiling and giving him tips on college . . . no idea in the world that I am paying for all of this . . . what I haven't been able to cover through grants or stipends or a work-study job . . . the rest is coming from me and will for the next four years . . . more lies as I sign over checks or steal away cash from our shared accounts . . . all the ways in which I've promised to help Tommy . . . and in this moment Tommy knows that we share something here that no one else knows about . . . not one other person . . . and I can feel him puff up with the pleasure of that . . . that power . . . staring right into Eric's eyes . . . smiling at him. (*Beat.*) He never introduces us

to the girl . . . she hangs back a bit, looking at things on her phone
. . . as Tommy goes on and on, telling Eric how "great" his wife is
and what a "lifesaver" she's been . . . helping a "young man like
me" get to college and out of his terrible family situation . . . all of
it. Word by word. Soaking in the moment . . . taking his time while
I try to make excuses for us to leave . . . (*Beat.*) And at some point
. . . he glances back at me. At my face. And I try to stay calm,
I do . . . to not panic . . . but my hands—I've thought about this a
million times since then . . . at least that . . . one *million* times . . .
if only I hadn't moved so quickly . . . my hands darting down to
my stomach, covering it. But I do . . . and he sees this . . . Tommy
does . . . and follows the movement down, studying me, surveying
my body, and it's then that he sees the gentle rise of my belly . . .
the bags in my hands from *Baby Gap* and *The Pottery Barn* . . .
spilling over with lamp shades and blankets and . . . and he slowly
lifts his head and looks at me. Stops speaking entirely and just
. . . stares at me for what feels like . . . well . . . forever, I suppose.
Ten seconds, maybe, in reality but forever as I see his flickering
eyes and his mind working as he counts off the weeks and the
months and remembers me whispering things to him, about my
life, about Eric and me, about all the difficulties we've had with
having children . . . and there, in the middle of the Glenview Mall
. . . he realizes the truth. Whose baby I am carrying and what has
transpired between us—why and for how long he has been used
and deceived and lied to—he now understands it all. (*Beat.*)
Tommy turns back to Eric and he smiles. Slowly. Baring his teeth.
He says, "I congratulate you, sir, on your upcoming arrival." It
couldn't have sounded more unnatural coming out of his mouth
than if one of those schoolboys from the *Lord of the Flies* had
suddenly appeared and said that very same thing. "Your upcom-

ing arrival." My God! (*Beat.*) Tommy said "goodbye" very quickly and left . . . the girl following him off into the maze of that mall . . . and Eric and I walked out to the car without speaking. (*Beat.*) Did Eric know? Could he feel it, the truth of what had just happened? Impossible to say. (*Beat.*) I catch Eric looking at me sometimes, with that . . . you know what I mean . . . and I believe he knows. Everything. And yet Eric's been a wonderful father to our daughter. A daughter who was born prematurely at 6 pounds and 3 ounces and has cried and fussed her way through those first few years of her life . . . I mean, not when she is in Eric's arms, no, then she's just perfect . . . an angel . . . but she has never once felt comfortable in my own arms. She's grown up a fussy child—a fussy eater, a fussy dresser, a fussy everything—and now, in her teenage years . . . she and I grow more distant with each passing day. For comfort I read articles in magazines that say this is a "phase" and that she'll "grow out of it" but I have my doubts. She is willful and short with me . . . she is her daddy's daughter and Eric spoils her without care or mercy . . . they whisper to each other and do things together that make me feel alone . . . the one gift that I wished to give him in this life has turned on me like a thistle in a garden . . . and there is *nothing* I can do. Now or ever. To say anything would be to say everything. She is the very picture of her father—not *Eric*, her *father*—and so it goes. This is what I've done . . . this is the cost of my lust and my treachery and my duplicity. (*Beat.*) And what of Tommy? You might well ask . . . as I mentioned, he has a good job just outside Chicago in IT. For a large supermarket chain of some sort . . . Wal-Mart, or am I completely wrong about that . . .? (*Shrugs.*) Lately, my daughter has been . . . in contact with someone. (*Beat.*) Some person who emails her and texts her and whom I can hear her talking to and giggling with through her bedroom walls . . . if I ask who it is, I'm shouted at or laughed at or belittled in such a way that I can get no information out of her . . . and if I talk to Eric on the subject, then he sides with her and just brushes my fears away. (*Beat.*) Because they can only be the fears of a mother and nothing more, is what he believes. For what else *could* it be that frightens me and keeps me up all night? What *other* possibility can exist? Why would I *ever* imagine it to be some part of my past coming back to haunt me now rather than just some boy . . . a boy who simply wants to talk to our girl? A boy that my daughter has met at school or the mall or some- where else and he just wants to speak with her? This must be the case. It *must* be. Who else could it be? (*Beat.*) Who else indeed. (*Beat.*) And so now I wait . . . and wait . . . and sit and wait . . . listening in fear for the ring of the phone or for some email that will finally unravel this giant web of deceit that I have created. I wait while life exacts its sweet revenge . . . one tick . . . tock . . . tick . . . of the clock . . . at a time.

She is worked up now, near tears but trying to hold it all together.

I was—not long ago I ran into the girl whom I mentioned before. The one from earlier . . . who asked that question. Back in school. (*Beat.*) We're in line somewhere and as we shuffle along with the group . . . waiting our turns—just before I leave her side—I lean over to her and I whisper, "*6 pounds, 3 ounces . . . that was the weight of mine*" and she looks at me . . . this girl—now a woman, trying to place me, wondering who the hell this is, this person— she stares at me as if I am insane, and I probably am! I probably am. I mean . . . God knows what she's thinking, what she under- stands this to mean . . . and after all that's happened . . . *yes* . . . I may well be a crazy person, I very well may be . . . but *this* much

I do know . . . this much I now know for sure: the weight of a lie is *never* the same for any of us . . . not ever. No, each one is *unique* . . . each one is *special* . . . each one is and always will be its very own particular burden. (*Beat.*) And for me the weight of that lie is: 6 pounds, 3 ounces. 6 *pounds and* 3 *ounces . . . 6* pounds, *3* ounces . . . 6 pounds *and* 3 ounces . . . 6 pounds . . . 3 ounces . . .

She continues to say these numbers to herself now, over and over, in some kind of quiet mantra. Endlessly. In a voice that only she can hear.

Another one of those beautiful songs begins to play. Nina Simone or Peggy Lee. Someone like that.

The lights slowly fade away.

Silence. Darkness.

ALL MY WHITE SINS FORGIVEN

Silence. Darkness.

A stretch of grass near a public basketball court. A couple benches off to one side. Garbage can and drinking fountain.

Two men sitting on one of the benches. Drenched in sweat. A ball near their feet. One is coughing. The other smiling.

ERIC . . . get it out, man . . . get it out!

TODD (*Coughing.*) *Shut the fuck up!*

ERIC Getting old, my friend . . .

TODD Yeah, yeah . . .

ERIC You're getting on up there . . .

TODD Bullshit!

ERIC Well . . .

TODD I ran your ass all over that court this morning . . .

ERIC Not sure that's true . . .

TODD . . . ummmmmm . . .

ERIC What?

TODD Pretty much!

ERIC You won three games, bitch . . .

TODD Yeah, that's right! *Three!*

ERIC And I won two . . .

TODD Uh-huh . . . and that means I won, homie.

ERIC And two of the three you won were by, like . . . two points or some shit.

TODD Yeah, so . . .?

ERIC And mine were blow-outs. Both of 'em . . .

TODD Whatever.

ERIC I'm just saying . . .

TODD I'm just saying I won, nigga. Best of five . . . *so* . . .

ERIC Shut up.

TODD What?

ERIC "Nigga."

TODD What?

ERIC When did you start . . . when do you ever use that? Hmmm? "Nigga?"

TODD I have before . . .

ERIC When?

TODD Man, come on . . . I totally have!

ERIC I'm sure, but . . . not . . .

TODD What?

ERIC Not around me . . .

TODD Yes, I have!

ERIC *Okay.*

TODD Man . . . you're *such* a motherfucker . . .

TODD *laughs and elbows* ERIC. *He pulls a big bottle of some energy drink out of his bag. Slops some down. Offers it to* ERIC, *who takes a drink.*

ERIC Thanks.

TODD Welcome. (*Smiles.*) That's right . . . suck down those *electro-lites*!

ERIC Nice that your parents taught you to share . . .

TODD Ha! Yeah, well . . . that's about all they taught me . . .

ERIC Ha! Same. I mean . . . pretty much . . .

TODD Yeah. Parents fucking suck.

ERIC Not all, but . . .

TODD Lots.

ERIC Yeah. Dads, mostly.

TODD Moms, too. Trust me.

ERIC Sure. (*Beat.*) Dads in my case . . .

TODD Got it. (*Beat.*) More than one . . .?

ERIC Oh yeah.

TODD Understood.

ERIC Yep. (*Beat.*) My moms had a couple . . . I guess she kept thinking she'd get it right at some point but you know what? She never did . . .

TODD I feel you, my brother.

ERIC Thanks, man.

ERIC *gets up, stretching out one knee. He picks up the ball and dribbles a bit. He's not bad at it. Between the knees and around the back.*

TODD You got skills—I'll give you that.

ERIC Thank you kindly.

TODD I mean, for a bitch who just got played . . . you got mad skills.

ERIC Ha!

TODD That's right . . .

ERIC You mean, a "bitch nigga," don't you . . .?

TODD Ha! That's exactly right—some lil' bitch ass nigga.

The two men smile at this and pass the ball back and forth a few times. Harder and harder. Finally, they stop.

ERIC Seriously, though . . .

TODD Yeah, what?

ERIC The "nigga" thing. You don't do it much . . . do you? I really never have heard you say that . . .

TODD I do every so often. Around another brother or that kinda thing—when a circumstance allows.

ERIC Got it.

TODD When it feels right . . .

ERIC Okay.

TODD You don't?

ERIC Not really . . .

TODD No?

ERIC Uh-uh.

TODD Never?

ERIC . . .

TODD Interesting.

ERIC Not really . . . I just don't. I'm not judging . . .

TODD Yeah?

ERIC Absolutely not.

TODD Hmmmm.

ERIC I'm seriously not. I never would . . .

TODD Cool.

ERIC I just . . .

TODD Yeah! Here it comes . . .

ERIC No! I'm only saying that . . . for me, it's never sounded right in my head or . . . like . . . my mouth . . . times I have said it . . . into a mirror or whatnot.

TODD You've *practiced?*

ERIC Shut the fuck up, dick!

TODD Ha! I love that . . . everybody at the office is gonna hear that shit now!

ERIC Prick.

TODD "Eric Johnson is working his way up to saying 'nigga' on occasion . . ."

ERIC Fuck you, Todd.

TODD Ha!

ERIC . . .

TODD I hope you call me one first. I'd love that shit . . . break your *nigga* cherry on me! Please oh please!!

He slaps at his friend's face but ERIC *counters. They box each other for a moment. Smiling as they go.*

ERIC There's almost a hundred percent chance that your fucking wish is gonna come true . . . asshole.

TODD Ha!

ERIC *laughs along with his friend. He's still up and he picks up the ball and gets going with it again. Dribbling it.*

TODD *gets up and starts to block him, trying to take it away from him.*

The two men fight it out. Rough-housing. The possession of the ball become the most important thing in the world now.

ERIC Come on now . . . come on . . .

TODD Watch out . . . gimme that fucking . . .

ERIC You can't do this . . . you can't move like this . . .

TODD You slick motherfucker . . .!

ERIC Boom!

ERIC *jumps, faking a shot. Imagines it going in the hoop and through. Swish!*

They stop and laugh together. Bumping up against each other.

TODD You wanna go play another game or two?

ERIC If you wanna . . .

TODD Yeah, maybe. In a minute . . .

ERIC You're getting old, friend.

TODD Fuck that.

ERIC Like an old dog . . .

TODD Still got game . . . you know that's true . . .

ERIC Yeah, you do. You got some.

TODD You, too.

ERIC Yeah, for a middle-aged man . . . yes, I do . . .

TODD For a half-baked middle-aged man . . . don't forget that part.

ERIC Right!

TODD You're not even real . . . not a full-fledged brother with all those . . . you know . . . extra muscles bred into your legs and all that shit. You ain't even got that!

ERIC That is too true . . .

TODD You better believe it. *Nigga.*

They both laugh at this and sit back down. ERIC *continues to dribble the ball while he sits.*

 . . . mixed-race motherfucker . . .

ERIC That's me! (*Laughs.*) That is who I am . . .

TODD Yep. With all them . . . you know . . . fine white features . . .

ERIC That's true. Look at my nose. It's very handsome.

TODD You're like Denzel or some shit . . .

ERIC No, *please* . . . better than that . . . way better than that!

TODD What, you talking . . .?

ERIC I'm talking me some Poitier-looking features over here . . .

TODD Ha! That is kinda true . . .

ERIC Chiseled and some shit . . .

TODD You and Barack . . .

ERIC Fuck no! I'm *way* more pretty than Barack! Way more . . .

TODD Yeah . . . from behind, maybe . . .

ERIC Asshole.

TODD Seriously, though . . . that's a pretty good-looking black man . . .

ERIC He's not black.

TODD Who's not?

ERIC The president. Obama.

TODD *What?*

ERIC He's mixed. Like me. That's not black . . .

TODD *looks at* ERIC *and shakes his head, laughing at this.*

TODD Dude, shut the fuck up . . .

ERIC He's not! I mean, we've decided that he is . . . appropriated him in that way, but come on . . .

TODD You're crazy . . . Obama is black . . .! We've got a black president.

ERIC We've got a mixed president. Just as white as he is black . . .

TODD That's a fucking . . .

ERIC It's the truth.

TODD Whatever.

ERIC You know it is . . .

TODD No!

ERIC Todd, come on . . .

TODD I mean . . . yes, he's mixed. That's true, but he has grown up accepting his blackness . . .

ERIC That's fine . . .

TODD He's *embraced* it . . . married a black woman . . . spent his time around his black family . . . community . . . (*Beat.*) Unlike *someone* I know . . .

ERIC Fuck you. (*Beat.*) *Anyway*, doesn't make him black.

TODD Yeah, but . . . all of his . . .

ERIC I'm just saying.

TODD Yeah. I hear ya . . . *but* . . .

They stop at this point; better just to let this go for now and so they do.

Another dribble of the ball. Another sip of Gatorade.

ERIC Anyway . . . if I look like an Obama, it's not Barack . . . it's Michelle.

TODD Ha!

ERIC It's true! I'm as pretty as she is.

TODD Fuck you are! That woman is fine . . .

ERIC Those *arms* . . .

TODD Fuck . . . me . . . those arms are special.

ERIC I give you that . . .

TODD Ummmmm! Fuck those fucking arms . . .

ERIC Oh yeah. That woman looks good in a fucking sleeveless top . . .

TODD Agreed. (*Beat.*) Perfect arms.

They think about this for a moment, both nodding their heads. After a moment, TODD *checks his watch.*

ERIC You gotta go?

TODD Yeah. Pretty soon . . .

ERIC Got it.

ERIC *glances at his friend, then off into the distance.*

   . . . so how's Karen? She good?

TODD Sure.

ERIC Ha! I guess that's an answer . . .

TODD Only one you're gonna get!

ERIC Ha! I'm fine with that . . . you guys do your thing, none of my business.

TODD That's true. (*Beat.*) And Faye? She's okay?

ERIC Yep.

TODD Ha!

ERIC Shut the fuck up . . . Faye is great.

TODD I bet.

ERIC She *is*! (*Beat.*) We seriously are . . . we're doing very well. Better than ever.

TODD Then awesome.

ERIC Whatever . . .

TODD *laughs and elbows* TODD. TODD *fights back and pretty soon the two men are pushing and shoving each other in a mock fight.*

ERIC *ends up pinned under* TODD's *arm and has to slap him on the arm repeatedly to get him to stop.*

TODD *finally does. Releases* ERIC *and* ERIC *sits up. Punches* TODD *in the arm one time.* TODD *smiles over at his friend.*

TODD Bitch.

ERIC Look who's talking . . . bitch.

TODD *sits for a moment, looking out.* ERIC *watches him and turns to see what he's looking at. Turns back and says:*

How're the kids?

TODD Real good.

ERIC Nice.

TODD Yeah. TJ is doing great in track . . . running the 100. And hurdles.

ERIC Excellent!

TODD And Shayleen is . . . you know . . . doing her thing, too.

ERIC Yeah?

TODD Sure. Loves *reading* and shit. She's in some little book club at school and volunteers at the library . . .

ERIC That's nice. (*Beat.*) Tracy does too . . .

TODD Got Shayleen into these riding lessons—like, on a *horse*— every other weekend, so that's . . . you know . . . not a "sport" exactly . . . but something . . .

ERIC Right.

TODD Girls aren't like boys . . . you know?

ERIC . . .

TODD Sorry. I just meant . . .

ERIC Don't worry about it.

TODD Yeah, but . . . anyway. Sorry.

ERIC I know what you mean . . .

TODD It's just . . . they like all kinds 'a shit. That's all.

ERIC That's true.

The two men sit there for another minute. Smile at each other. TODD *pats* ERIC *on the thigh without looking.*

Thanks, *nigga.*

TODD *laughs at this and punches* ERIC *in the arm.* ERIC *puts a hand to his shoulder and pretends to winch.*

TODD *laughs and hits him again.* ERIC *punches him back this time.*

Another moment of quiet between them.

Finally:

. . . you ever . . .?

TODD What?

ERIC Nah. Nothing.

TODD Asshole . . . *what*?

ERIC . . .

TODD Just say it.

ERIC *struggles to put into words what he's feeling.*

ERIC I'm not even . . . I dunno . . .

TODD Dude, come *on*!

ERIC I don't know! (*Beat.*) I'm just sort of . . . you know . . . feeling something. These days. (*Beat.*) Whatever.

TODD Man, that's everyday for me . . .

ERIC Yeah?

TODD Fuck yes. And that's on a *good* day.

ERIC Huh.

TODD Everybody feels that . . .

ERIC Okay.

TODD It's true.

ERIC No, yeah . . . I believe you . . .

TODD Alright then . . .

ERIC But . . . I mean . . . what is it? (*Beat.*) That feeling?

TODD Fuck if I know! Something.

ERIC "Something."

TODD Yup.

ERIC Well, that's helpful. (*Laughs.*) I mean . . . *fuck* . . .

TODD Exactly!

ERIC I feel like . . . I'm not sure . . . if Faye and I, if we'd had kids earlier—earlier in our life together, I'm saying, or more than just one . . . a *boy*, maybe—then it'd be different. Somehow.

TODD Yeah?

ERIC I mean . . . probably . . . sure. Why not?

TODD No, you're probably right . . .

ERIC They just . . . you know? They *focus* you in a certain way . . .

TODD That they do!

ERIC You turn your attention to 'em and you just . . . you chug along, because of them. No matter what.

TODD That's kinda true.

ERIC *Right*? And you . . . whatever . . . doesn't mean you can't still fuck up, that you don't make mistakes or . . . you know . . . fall out of love with their mother or cheat on a person . . . kids don't make you perfect . . .

TODD Absolutely not! Not my two . . .

ERIC Exactly . . . but . . . I have kinda always believed that they do make you at least "better" . . . in a way. (*Beat.*) I believe that. (*Beat.*) They make you "better."

TODD Yeah . . . probably . . .

ERIC You see that at all? With TJ or . . . you know . . . Shayleen even?

TODD Maybe . . . yeah. Maybe so.

ERIC Huh.

TODD Like . . . sometimes I look at 'em . . . my kids, I'm saying . . . and I see a kind of . . . *finer* version of me. In them.

ERIC "Finer?"

TODD I dunno! Probably just because they look . . . they're younger and they've got . . . whatever . . . a newer insight on shit—technology and politics and . . . just . . . emotions, even. They can accept people for who they are and . . . I mean, my kid sees some ugly chick with these, like, little bits of metal stuck in her face . . . and he is okay with that. Thinks that it's "cool." And I mean, this is a *dog,* a very homely girl we're speaking about . . . with jewels, *in* her face . . . and it's all about "live and let live." (*Beat.*) And that's good. I personally still think she's a fucking *mutt*—I'd never touch her, if I was his age—but the fact that he likes her, accepts her for who she wants to be or is searching to be . . . that's better, right? He is becoming a more refined person than I am or will probably ever be . . .

ERIC Yeah. Maybe so. (*Beat.*) My Tracy is pretty perfect . . .

TODD   Yeah. And look at 'em . . . my kids . . . they can be whatever they wanna be now. These days? It's wide open. Even the fucking *President* if they're interested in that . . . now it's a possibility at least.

ERIC   That's true.

TODD   Yep. (*Smiles.*) My kid could be the *first* black president . . . right?

ERIC   Ha! Yeah, that's true . . .

TODD   I mean, after that mixed motherfucker we got in there now . . .

ERIC   He *is*, bitch! Motherfucker's white as I am . . .

TODD   Yeah, whatever . . .

ERIC   Fuck you.

TODD   Fuck yourself, smart boy.

ERIC *laughs this off, then starts to kick at the basketball again. Moving it back and forth, like a soccer player.*

Soon TODD *is involved, remaining seated but trying to take the ball away from* ERIC.

They sit next to each other, grappling with one another in their quest to possess the ball.

Elbows fly and they push and shove as ERIC *works to keep the ball from* TODD. TODD *finally gets control and* ERIC *lunges at him.*

TODD *stands up, victorious and* ERIC *falls over onto his side.*

ERIC   Fuck!

TODD   Yes!

ERIC   Bastard!!

TODD   Oh yeah!!

ERIC   (*Standing up.*) You wanna go play another couple games before we go back . . .?

TODD Wish I could . . .

ERIC Yeah, no . . . I get it.

TODD I got the kids this morning. Karen is off at some thing she's
got . . .

ERIC "Thing?"

TODD You know . . . a "lady" thing. Some *gathering* . . . with lunch.

ERIC Ahhh. Like that.

TODD Yep. (*Beat.*) Faye do that sorta thing? Crap like that? *Gather*
with other ladies . . .?

ERIC Sure. Sometimes.

TODD Huh.

ERIC A lot of shit with school and . . . you know . . . the PTA and
stuff like that . . .

TODD Right.

ERIC Helping kids . . . she does a bunch of that college prep shit, for
those tests they take . . . remember?

TODD Like SATs and whatever?

ERIC Yeah! Like that . . .

TODD That's cool . . .

ERIC Yep. When she spots someone with a gift or, like, in drama—
some very talented boy or girl—she'll make it her . . . *thing* . . .
to get them some kind of scholarship or that type of deal . . .

TODD Solid. I like that.

ERIC Yeah, she's amazing . . . really gets behind them and pushes
and . . . you know . . . makes a difference in their lives . . .

TODD I bet.

ERIC Yeah.

TODD Awesome.

ERIC Yep. (*Beat.*) Faye. (*Beat.*) She's a really great person . . .

TODD Ha!

ERIC   What? (*Shoving* TODD.) WHAT?!

TODD   You sound like a *mayor . . .* talking about somebody who's in charge of the "flower show" this year . . .

ERIC   Fuck you, asshole!

TODD   You do!

ERIC   Dick.

ERIC *laughs at this while shoving his friend again. Hard.*

TODD   "She's a really great person . . ."

ERIC   Ha! Fuck off . . .

TODD   "She's just lovely . . ."

ERIC   Motherfucker . . . you *know* what I'm saying!

TODD   Yeah, I do . . . I'm kidding . . .

ERIC   Alright, then.

TODD   Ha!

ERIC   Fucker. (*Smiles.*) Been with the same woman for twenty some years, so . . . gimme a fucking break.

TODD   Truth.

ERIC   Yeah . . . and . . . she's beautiful . . . Faye is everything to me, we have a very good life together . . .

TODD   But?

ERIC   "But" what?

TODD   You don't have a lead-in like that without "but" coming hard and fast 'round the corner . . .

ERIC   Is that right?

TODD   That is very right, my friend . . .

ERIC   Yeah, well . . .

ERIC *thinks about this for a moment. Picks up the ball and bounces it. Looks at his friend. Keeps bouncing that ball.*

In a perfect world?

TODD What?

ERIC Would I be there . . . with her . . . in a perfect world?

TODD You tell me . . .

ERIC I mean . . . obviously . . . I wouldn't be using that phrase if
   I thought me being with her was perfect. Then I wouldn't say
   that—"perfect world." I'd just say life with her was . . . you know
   . . . "perfect" and that'd be that. (*Beat.*) Right?

TODD . . . I guess . . .

ERIC Of *course* I would. (*Beat.*) Yes.

TODD So . . . then . . .?

ERIC *Dude.*

TODD You started this shit! (*Beat.*) So . . .

ERIC I like my job. I like this. Hanging out here . . . with you. (*Beat.*)
   I like it.

TODD Thank you, brother.

ERIC I do. (*Beat.*) And we got a nice big house . . . I like my
   Lexus, that's a nice car . . . I *love* my daughter . . . BUT; yeah,
   you're right, BUT: is this who I am? Where I can see myself in
   my dream of dreams, whatever-the-fuck that even means?
   No. Probably not . . .

TODD So . . . then . . . what? (*Beat.*) Eric?

ERIC I don't even know . . .

TODD Bullshit.

ERIC I don't!

TODD Yes, you do . . .

ERIC Oh, really?

TODD I mean . . . probably . . . if you were honest with yourself . . .

ERIC . . .

TODD I'm just saying . . .

ERIC Huh. (*Beat.*) And YOU do?

TODD Sure. I got a secret me . . . a "me" that I'd rather be
. . . *'course* I do!

ERIC You do?

TODD Totally.

ERIC And you wanna tell me what that is, or . . .?

TODD Not in a *million* goddamn years . . .

ERIC Of course!

TODD Obviously . . .

ERIC But you do have one . . .?

TODD I absolutely do.

ERIC Huh.

TODD Yep.

ERIC Would I be surprised . . .?

TODD . . . *by* . . .?

ERIC What it is . . . who you'd be. If you could be that thing . . .

TODD Probably. (*Beat.*) I could, though. Any time. Be it.

ERIC Yeah?

TODD Of course. Take me six hours to do it . . . if I had the balls . . .

ERIC Jesus.

TODD I mean . . . that's probably . . . a couple days, maybe, but
that's about it.

ERIC *Yeah?*

TODD Yep.

ERIC And all this time . . . since I've know you and, like . . . you've
been married and had kids . . . all this time you've wanted this
other thing? This life you don't live . . .?

TODD No.

ERIC Oh. So . . . then . . .?

TODD Along the way. I figured it out.

ERIC But it's . . . what?

TODD You know . . .

ERIC No, what?

TODD Dude! It's too late . . . can't happen now. (*Beat.*) So. There.

ERIC Oh.

TODD I made . . . you know . . . commitments and shit like that.
    To be *this* guy. Who I am now.

ERIC Yeah, but people . . . they can . . .

TODD Not me.

ERIC Alright.

TODD I could never do that. Not to TJ.

ERIC Or Shayleen . . .

TODD No. Her, either.

ERIC I see. I get that. (*Beat.*) I totally get it . . .

TODD *nods and checks his watch again. A glance over at his friend.*

TODD Yep. (*Beat.*) But you . . . you know . . . whatever . . . you
    could probably . . . you *know.* (*Beat.*) I'm just saying . . .

ERIC What?

TODD Nothing. (*Beat.*) Just . . . you're braver than me that way . . .

ERIC No, bro, come on . . . same thing . . .

TODD What? *How*?

ERIC With Faye. (*Beat.*) *Please.*

TODD No, that's not the same . . .

ERIC I'm not saying that. I'm not saying it's *the* very same, but . . .
    it kinda amounts to the same. Pretty much.

TODD I guess.

ERIC For me it does . . . (*Beat.*) It'd kill her. Seriously. (*Beat.*) If
    I left . . .

TODD Yeah?

ERIC *Yes.* No question.

TODD You might be surprised . . .

ERIC Why do you say that?

TODD . . . just . . .

ERIC No, why? *Tell* me . . .

TODD 'Cause . . . listen to us, with these people that we'd rather be . . . these secret lives that we'd wanna have if we could . . . who says she's not the very same way . . .?

ERIC . . . no . . .

TODD I'm just saying.

ERIC Yeah? (*Beat.*) You think?

TODD It's possible . . . that's all that I'm saying . . .

ERIC But . . . no. I'm like you. It's, like, way too late . . .

TODD Maybe. Maybe so . . . only one kid, though.

ERIC And even if I did, I don't even know what I'd . . . I mean, I guess I'd be one or the other . . . black or white, not like I am now . . . caught in the middle . . . but that's . . .

TODD Yeah?

ERIC Probably. Why not? (*Beat.*) Get all my white sins forgiven, or . . . you know . . . go the other way, even. A *Black Panther* or some shit. Fighting the good fight. (*Beat.*) On one side or the other . . .

TODD Yeah? That's what you'd do . . .?

ERIC I said I don't even know . . . (*Beat.*) But yeah. Maybe.

TODD *thinks about this, taking his friend in. With maybe even a greater appreciation of him than he ever had before.*

TODD I know Karen would. In two seconds.

ERIC *Really*?

TODD Nigga, please . . .

ERIC Ha!

TODD I'm not even kidding . . .

ERIC Wow.

TODD Yep. (*Beat.*) Just the way it is.

ERIC And . . . do you know what she'd be? If she could?

TODD Nah . . . I dunno . . . I mean, maybe. Some kinda . . . business person. Like me . . . but not tied down by family. She'd travel and shit. Fuck Asian guys . . . she's attracted to *Asian* guys, you believe that?

ERIC *What?*

TODD I'm just . . . over the course of time, you pick up these things . . . and I've discovered that. Asian dudes. Bruce Lee. His kid. A newscaster guy they have on ABC. (*Beat.*) That one dude on *The Walking Dead.* (*Beat.*) It adds up . . .

ERIC Yeah. I guess so . . .

TODD But she's not gonna. She won't be leaving me or fucking those guys. Uh-uh. It's not gonna happen . . . (*Beat.*) It's just a thing I think she'd do . . . *if* she got the chance.

ERIC I see.

TODD Same as me . . .

ERIC Asian guys?

TODD *Motherfucker . . .*

ERIC Kidding! (*Changing subjects.*) Your "thing," you mean . . . which you won't tell me about. (*Beat.*) If you got a chance . . . you'd run off and do that, or be that other person . . . right? If you could . . .

TODD . . . and I wasn't hurting my kids or anything like that . . .?

ERIC Right . . . exactly . . .

TODD Then yeah. There's a pretty decent chance I would. (*Beat.*) *Yes.*

ERIC Huh.

TODD I mean, over fifty perfect I'd say, so that's fairly serious . . .

They think about this and bump elbows, throwing a few punches at each other. Bobbing and weaving.

Finally, they stop and TODD *checks his watch. Again.*

    I should get going, bro . . .

ERIC Cool.

TODD See you next Saturday?

ERIC Absolutely . . . I mean . . . *and* at work.

TODD Oh, right. True. (*Beat.*) Duh.

ERIC Alright, good. Thanks, man . . .

TODD You got it, *nigga.*

ERIC Dude . . .

TODD I'm joking! Fuck! *Relax* . . .

ERIC Alright, whatever. I'll see ya.

TODD You too.

ERIC Great.

TODD You taking off soon, or . . .?

ERIC Nah . . . Faye has one of her things today . . . you know . . . what I said . . . her college prep things. With some kid. (*Beat.*) She uses the basement office and it gives me a few hours to do my thing . . . since all Tracy wants to do is sit on the Internet the whole weekend . . .

TODD Huh.

ERIC Yeah . . . I think I'm just gonna hang out here . . . maybe do a pick-up game or something . . . see who's around . . .

TODD Nice. (*Walking off.*) Enjoy!

ERIC Thanks, man!

TODD You got it, brother . . .

TODD *picks up his stuff—a gym bag and a towel, a drink bottle, etc.— bundles it together and heads off toward a parking lot in the distance.*

ERIC *watches him go. One last nod of the head and a smile as his friend disappears from view.*

ERIC *stretches, looks at his own watch, then picks up the basketball and starts to dribble.*

He moves in more elaborate patterns as he works at it. The ball spins and moves through the air as if it were magic.

ERIC *concentrates as he bounces the ball, playing a game in his mind in which he is a star and he can do no wrong.*

ERIC   (*To himself.*) . . . there he goes . . . there he goes . . . he's unstoppable today . . . he's up and down the court, without even touching the parquet . . . from downtown, in the paint . . . it does not matter, he's on fire today . . . Eric Johnson is absolutely on fire . . . oh, and that's a *three*! He is *un*-believable!! With two seconds left on the clock, Johnson has brought his team back to within one . . . it's his fifth triple-double of the season and he's absolutely . . . he's stolen the ball! He's got the ball and he's moving toward the basket . . . past one defender, now another . . . this is just . . . the crowd goes wild!! Listen to them!! LISTEN TO THEM!! The . . . crowd . . . is . . . going . . . wild . . . !

The imaginary crowd sounds grow and grow, overtaking us and drowning out all other sound.

The lights brighten in intensity until ERIC *is nothing more than a ripple of movement in a sea of white.*

The crowd continues to roar its imaginary approval.

Silence. Darkness.

WITH HAIR OF HAND-SPUN GOLD

I'M BACK.

I am back and you knew I would be. You knew it. Didn't you? Yes, you did, don't give me that look, you knew exactly what was going to—doesn't matter. I'm here now so we should get started, get this thing all started and going. Go ahead, you can throw up, it's not going to stop me, make me feel bad, I promise you. It's not. You're getting exactly what you deserve here, you are, you deserve it and that's what is going to happen. Fate, or Karma or, or whatever they call it. Kismet? I know that was a play or something, a musical, but I think that word means the same sort of thing. Something happening that was supposed to happen and then it does. It comes true. Wham! Just like that. "Instant Karma," isn't that what Lennon called it? Not the dictator, but the Beatles guy. In his song. Right? He said "it's gonna get you" and that is just so goddamn true. It reaches out—figures out where you are, takes its time to find you—and bam! Before you can even move or anything, it's got you by the throat and you are fucked. It's true, my dear. You are motherfucked. And so that's you, today, at this very minute. Or second, or whatever you wanna call it. You are about to be motherfucked. By me.

I can see by the look on your face you're surprised, so don't pretend. Do not pretend that you were ready for this one because you weren't. You were not. I came out of the blue, as they like to say, out of the darkness like some avenging angel—I'm not sure that's the exact right analogy but you get what I mean—I appeared and it has thrown you for a loop. A big ol' loop and you don't know what to do, what to say even, sitting there on a park bench with your mouth hanging open and staring at me. Wow. I really caught you off guard, didn't I? You knew this could happen but you still were not ready for it. Not today. Well, I can't say that it doesn't make me happy because it does. It makes me smile right down into my soul and that's the truth so you might as well know it. I am happy to see you sweat. Really. Honestly I am. I mean, who knew? How would I ever know that it'd be this easy to make that happen, to bring your little world to a halt, for it to come crashing down around your ears? How could I be privy to a thing like that? You can't, that's the answer. You wouldn't until you just go ahead and do it and now I have and I'm aware, by looking at your face I'm aware of the magnitude of what's going on right now, at this moment, as we sit here quietly in the middle of this park and your kid is playing on the swings and life bounces merrily along. If you could scream or draw a gun or kill me even, stab me and cover me with dirt right here in those bushes behind us, I think you would. I know it, actually. I know that you would. And, to be fair, I might do the same damn thing if I was you, shoe on the other foot or whatever people say to mean what I'm talking about. I might also want to do you harm. Well, I do, actually, want that, me, I'm saying, shoe on my own foot and staring at you right now. I do want to bring a kind of harm to your life. And I'm about to. Yes, I am. Yes indeed.

Did you ever think, I mean, years ago, when you first saw me— picked me out of some gym class as the one you wanted—could you ever even imagine that it might come to this? I can't believe that you would've, right? No, never, not in a million years or you probably wouldn't have done it, that's what I think. That has to be the truth because, I mean, why would you otherwise? You know? Yeah. It's true. You wouldn't. No, I was supposed to be a good boy, do what you say, nod when you ask, and that was going to be that. Easy as pie, that's the phrase. My mom uses it—still, to this day—and it fits and so that's why we say it, why I just said it now. Because it's true. You planned on using and discarding me along the way without my ever knowing it. As easy as pie. And you did, to be fair, you got away with it for a really long time. True? I mean, a good long time. Right up until about seven months ago and that, my dear, is a hell of a run.

Nice long run. You shouldn't look so nervous because you gave it a real go so that's at least something. And look, it's not like I plan on telling anybody, I really don't, I mean, who could I tell? Who? Hmm? I mean, who would ever believe a story like this one?

I don't mind that you're black, I don't, I've always been attracted to black women. Well, not necessarily black but darker-skinned people. Girls with tans and that sort of thing. And you were definitely that, which stood out at our school, didn't it? You certainly did. Talk of the town, some might say, a real object of interest and I'm sure a few of those men you worked with—teachers and coaches and administrators—they probably found you rather exotic and worth chatting up in the lounge. I'm sure it happened, I know it did, in fact, because I would see you often from where I sat in the office, waiting to get yelled at again by the vice principal. What was that jerk's name, I don't remember now. It doesn't matter, he died years ago from cancer—one of the bad ones, like bowel or brain or something—and I recall not feeling a thing when I heard that news. Maybe even said "good" under my breath or smiled or something. Not instant, but karma. But you didn't talk to those men, did you, my dear, because you were already married, already wrapped up in a relationship and so you made a choice, you picked me out of the crowd—maybe there in the office rather than gym class, now that I think about it, maybe so—and said to yourself that I was the one. The worthwhile one, the one to play with and drive wild with desire. I know you helped me, too, I know that, gave me a belief in myself and pushed me to study and try and get into junior college even, you did all that and I appreciate it, I do, but all the while you made me feel like I was your boy. The guy you wanted in your life, if only your husband wasn't around, if only things were different. If only. And I believed you, oh how I gobbled up the shit you spewed, gobbled it up and swallowed it down and smiled at you in the hall and from the bleachers and as you drove off in your dirty yellow bug on your way home each night. I believed you and loved you and gave you my little teenage heart there at West Valley High and I've never done that again, no, not ever, I haven't. To anyone ever ever ever again because my trust is gone, disappeared like you did the next year to a new school with the whisper of "it could never work" and "this is a real opportunity for me" and it was like you never existed. An empty office was your vapor trail (cutbacks didn't bring another of your kind, a counselor, into school until my senior year). Your desk and chair, alone in the dark was where I would eat my lunch most days unless they caught me and threw me out—that was all that was left of our love and time together. And there was love, wasn't there? Real, abiding love. I swear there was. Look at me right now and tell me there was and I will go away, leave you to watch your little girl as she runs about in the bright sunshine and I'll be gone. Say it, just once, say it to me now and mean it, while I sit here with you. I beg you. Go on.

You can't, can you? No, of course you can't because it's not true and you wouldn't want to lie about that, lead me on or anything, now, would you? Absolutely not. Part of the strange, strict principles by which you live your life, even though our entire union was absolutely that. A pure and utter lie, one that you lived so easily and without remorse for so long. That's hardly fair, though, is it, because how could I know your feelings about me at that time? That's a good point and I stand corrected or sit corrected, actually, sit corrected here on this bench with you. I-sit-corrected. Perhaps you did love me once, a while ago, a long, long time ago when I was sixteen and just learning to drive and we would meet off in the woods or at your home on an unexpected morning and make love. Yes, love, I'm sure it was, only that, never just fucking and you taught me everything I know about that undiscovered country. It was well beyond description and nothing I plan to embarrass you with right now, not in front of your daughter as she plays, but it was something lovely and I remember it like it was just yesterday even though a decade or so has slipped away. Lying there, inside of you and looking into your eyes, the quiet of a forest above us and your beautiful skin soaking up the sun, kissing that mouth of yours, those lips that sucked me in and devoured me,

I had no words for what you were doing to my life. And nothing now, now that I know the truth. The real truth of what we were doing there and why you loved me or said you did and watched me fall deeper and deeper into the endless chasm that was you.

Did I ever tell you that I imagined killing him? Your husband? Oh yes, so many times. When it was at its deepest and worst, the sickness of love made me want to be rid of him for all time and eternity. I planned his death, a dozen times, in various ways and done so successfully by me that even you believed that the car wreck or the mugging or hanging was a suicide or mistake or a simple twist of fate. And life goes on and I was suddenly with you always, at your side and we made a new life for ourselves in another state or country or on an island somewhere and the last that anyone ever saw of us was running, hand in hand, down the beach and off into that sunset people are always talking about. Yes. Was I wrong to think that? At the time I didn't feel I was, it felt justified by what you said about him, about your life together. Just phrases, really, a little clue tossed off now and again over a meal at A & W, some little comment that made me believe he didn't appreciate you, that he didn't want children with you or to grow old with you or anything any more, that you were trapped and alone and I was your savior, me, that only I could rescue you from the coal mine of a life that your marriage had become. Some white guy from home, a good family and a bad mistake is what you called it and I took it to heart, believed that his inability to father a child was of his own making rather than biology, that he was withholding from you and cold and distant and had even laid a finger—or more than that, a hand one time—on your sweet face that I had come to adore and would protect with my life. Did you know that at the time, that I would've done even that, died for you? Of course you did. Sixteen-year-olds can hide nothing. I was like some puppy chasing after you, big paws and tongue and silly and sweet. But you didn't want those things, did you? No, not all of them. Just one. One thing from me and when you had it you left so quickly, with such a fluttering of your wings that I was dazed and dazzled and I believed your whispers. I watched you drive away, even helped you pack your garage, if you can remember that, helped your husband pack up things into a U-Haul and swept it out and washed it down before you left. You paid me twenty dollars there in front of him, smiled at me like we'd never met and off I trotted, back home to wait for a call that never came and an address that was never, not ever, no, never sent.

And now you have your child, that thing you always said would make your life complete. Your husband, too, he got swept up in your miracle and never asked for a blood test that would tell him the horrid truth about you and your deeds. Your missteps. Your tiny plots. Instead you are a happy family living here, where I have found you and have now come to ask for something in return. Of course I have, don't look so surprised, my dear, for there is always a price to pay for things like this, when you have done what you have done and now the time has come.

All I want is nothing. That is, that nothing should change from this very moment on. I want you to know I know where you're at, who you are and what you've become. No, you didn't eventually divorce as you imagined to me you would, a life on your own in another city where I might join you one day, "when you're grown," you would say and oh how I believed you and your words. Those intoxicating words that spewed from your beautiful lips into my ear as I held you and hoped for such a day. But that day never came as you well know, it never did and on you stayed with your man—why wouldn't you, for there was never any plan on your part to leave him, to be alone, but to add, add a child to the mix and live happily ever after. My child. A child you took from me and I never even knew it. How clever of you, how smart and wily and clever. And almost perfect, the plan, it was almost the most perfect of plans but who knew that my sister—my stupid younger sister who I never really liked and I always thought was a little bit retarded—who could imagine that she could pass a course and would end up working for your doctor in town? You left no trace or so you thought, but files are files and so they stay and one nosy day she glanced inside to see that your husband, that man I was so ready to hate and kill and despise, she saw that he was empty and void and unable to provide and she thought this was interesting and said so to me and my family one evening out of the blue. They all recalled you fondly and thought it was a sad and strange tidbit about a lovely woman who had been so helpful to their son but I knew better, didn't I, my dear? I now knew that you had used me to become pregnant and then off you ran to hide your secret from the world. And me. The one who wanted to be your world but was really only a pawn. A sorry little pawn in your grisly and gory game of love.

But children grow up, God bless them, they do and reach out and up and try things all on their own, things that even their own parents don't always know about. And so I met your daughter, your little princess, on the Internet and have become her friend. What a place for people like us, you and I, the liars and braggarts and ghosts of this world. Such a nice place to hide and pretend and so I do, I am a lovely little teenage girl named "Samantha" with hair of hand-spun gold and I live in Texas with my family of five with our dog named "Bubbles" and a boyfriend named "Cory"—yes, I used your husband's name, I knew it would seal the deal when a squeal from your daughter was followed by "that's my dad's name, too! LOL!" Oh yes, she is mine for hours at a time now and we dream and talk and chatter on about a life together at college or beyond. It has been beautiful and filled with laughter and delight, not ugly like what you did to me, not wrong like how you used me. No. It has been so so beautiful and it needs to continue, must continue, and I know you have set restrictions on her recently because she gets online the second you leave the house and complains about you and so I know. But you will let her have this friend, won't you? Yes, or everything will be revealed. Do you understand me? All of it and to the end. I will ruin you and your perfect little fairy tale life if you stop her from seeing me. Obviously I can never meet her or tell her the truth, one day she will drift away from me and that will be that, as they say, I know this and accept it as fate. Kismet. Karma, not instant but destined and acceptable. But it is not for you to decide so stay away and so will I. That is the deal. That is the cost, my dear. She is yours, to be sure, but she is also mine now and mine she will stay. Yes. For as long as I can hold her she will be mine as well. Mine, mine, mine.

She's beautiful out there, isn't she? Dancing on the grass and running with her friends. I've had to send her photos of myself very carefully—using my little niece as a stand-in—but what I've seen of her has been no lie. She is perfect and golden and the one good thing to come out of the filthy ways you used me and soiled a part of my life. Don't look away because you know it's true. I hate women and their wily selves; I know men can suck and often do but you are a more treacherous creature overall, surely you recognize that as a truth. You ruined me and left me for dead. You built this burnished little life and happy little world on the shit and bones of my carcass without looking back—and now all I ask is that you continue to look away. Look off some other way when you see her sitting at the computer, giggling and talking with her "friends" on Facebook and Twitter and all the crap I've been reduced to just to be near her. My daughter. Look away, go into another room and leave us alone and by doing so your own rotten, deceitful life can exist for yet another day. Do you agree, my dear? Oh, how I hope so . . . here in my broken heart of hearts.

If you want me, need me, long for me as I do for you, my hated, hateful dear, you know where to find me. Out there, somewhere. Lost in space, on the world wide web. Rump69@hotmail.com.

I see you not looking at me. Head turned. Tears in your eyes. I so wish I knew what you were thinking but then again, I never really did, did I, so why would it matter now? And it doesn't. All that matters is you know the truth. Where we stand. And the truth of the matter is I'm here now. I am here and I'm not going away, no, I'm not. Not ever, my dear.

At least not for a very, very, very long time.

Neil LaBute burst onto the American theater scene with the premiere of BASH in 1999 in a wildly praised production that featured Calista Flockhart, Paul Rudd, and Ron Eldard. These three provocative one-act plays examine the complexities of evil in everyday life and exhibit LaBute's signature raw lyrical intensity. Ablaze with the muscular dialogue and searing artistry that immediately established him as a major playwright, BASH is enduringly brilliant—classic and essential Neil LaBute.

In MEDEA REDUX, a young woman relates her complex and ultimately tragic relationship with her high school English teacher; in IPHIGENIA IN OREM, a businessman confides to a stranger in a Las Vegas hotel room about a chilling crime; and in A GAGGLE OF SAINTS, a young couple separately recounts the violent events of an anniversary weekend in New York City,

This new edition has been produced with dual covers featuring two images, a man and a woman, from Robert Longo's acclaimed "Men in the Cities" series and includes an illuminating preface by Neil LaBute who for the first time limns the plays' full history, including the early productions and controversies during his student days.

"Mr. LaBute shows not only a merciless ear for contemporary speech but also a poet's sense of recurring, slyly graduated imagery . . . darkly engrossing." **—Ben Brantley, *The New York Times***

$14.95   978-1-58567-024-6

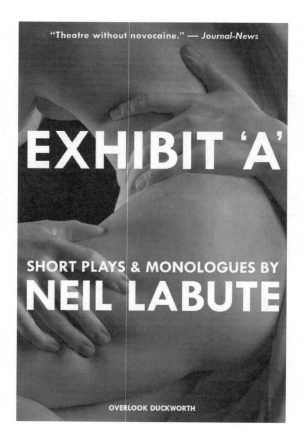

Neil LaBute has earned international acclaim for his provocative body of work for the stage. His bold vision is amply evident in this new collection of daring and stylishly realized short plays and monologues.

In the title play, *Exhibit 'A'*, an artist pushes the boundaries of his work to a previously untouched frontier, challenging the very definition of "art." *10K* explores the territory where fantasy and desire merge, as a man and woman share secrets while traversing a suburban jogging path. *Here We Go Round the Mulberry Bush* is a tense confrontation between two men in a park. In *Happy Hour*, a guy and a gal meet cute in a bar.

"LaBute takes us to shadowy places we don't like to talk about, sometimes even to think about."
—**Erin McClam,** *Newsday*

$17.95   978-1-4683-1319-2

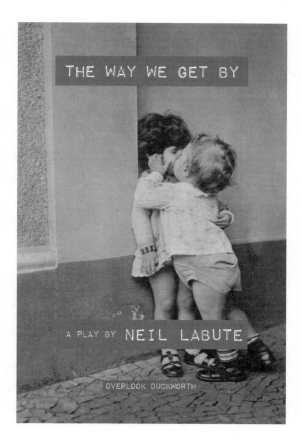

New York. Middle of the night. Now.

Meet Beth and Doug: two people who have no problem getting dates with their partners of choice. What they do have is an awkward encounter after spending one hit night together following a drunken wedding reception.

Slyly profound and irresistibly passionate, *The Way We Get By* is Neil LaBute's audacious tale of a very modern romance—a sharp, sexy, fresh look at love and lust and the whole damn thing.

"Viscerally romantic, almost shockingly sensitive, even, dare we say it, sweet . . . LaBute . . . dares here to explore less obviously explosive territory. Yet, somehow, this daring feels deep."   **—Linda Winer,** *Newsday*

$14.95 978-1-4683-1208-9

THE OVERLOOK PRESS • NEW YORK • WWW.OVERLOOKPRESS.COM

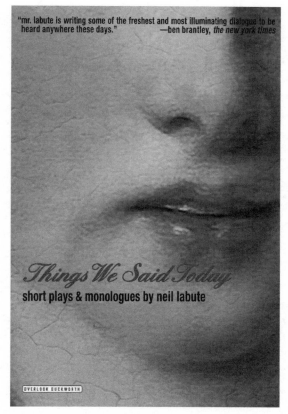

In this electrifying two-hander, the young and beautiful Velvet and the older, volatile Fred revisit a shared history, and as power shifts and tension mounts, the twisted heart of their relationship is slowly revealed in a stunning climax. This volume contains the stage version of this work, which is also a film directed by Neil LaBute, with Stanley Tucci and Alice Eve.

"*Some Velvet Morning* is provocation of the most artful kind." —*The Village Voice*

$14.95   978-1-4683-0916-4

THE OVERLOOK PRESS • NEW YORK • WWW.OVERLOOKPRESS.COM

Gen P
New Generation of Product Owners
Who Care About Customers

Joanna Tivig

Peter Monkhouse

1

Gen P
New Generation of Product Owners
Who Care About Customers

Joanna Tivig
Peter Monkhouse

4

About the Authors

Joanna Tivig, BA, CSPO
E: joanna@newgenp.com
L: https://www.linkedin.com/in/joanna-tivig-b877233/

Joanna is currently Co-Founder of Path2Knowledge, an organization providing online/in-class training and coaching services to executives and practice teams going through Agile and Digital transformations. Joanna consults half of her time for a digital startup called 'Y', with a focus on customer experience and digital transformation. As a part-time lecturer for the University of Toronto, School of Continuing Studies for over a decade, Joanna is teaching various courses to thousands of adult education students.

Joanna started her Canadian career managing projects in the financial services, working for Bank of Nova Scotia. By 2010, she had already become a Director of Mergers and Acquisitions, working on an acquisition in Puerto Rico. In 2012, Joanna became the Director of Enterprise Mobile Applications and continued to experiment and apply agile ways of working. Having worked with product teams who made an impact on customers, Joanna learned that the role of the product owner was crucial in delivering value for customers and organizations. As AVP, Digital Transformation for Investors Group, a role that she took on in 2015, Joanna has successfully built digital applications using Scrum, Kanban, and other frameworks and transformed the digital department into a self-managed, self-organizing, flat organization.

In January 2019, Joanna launched her first Agile product, called 2BVisual. It consists of custom design magnetic board and cards that bring ease of use and professionalism to Agile ways of working. The product has launched successfully and is beginning to penetrate the Canadian market while changing the way physical boards are being used.

Joanna is a committee member of the Toronto Agile Community since 2018 and one of the organizers of the Toronto Agile Conference (2018 and 2019), as well as Open Space event (2019). A believer in the power of community and the benefits of knowledge sharing, Joanna frequently participates as a guest speaker, panelist, or presenter at digital, agile and leadership events.

Joanna is determined to fight the battles of changing the cultures of organizations from control and command to commitment and serving, empowering product teams to prioritize the features that add the most value to customers.

Peter Monkhouse, MBA, PEng, PMP
E: peter@newgenp.com
L: https://www.linkedin.com/in/petermonkhouse

Peter is currently President of MonkArt, providing consulting and training services to organizations to help them implement their strategic plans. In addition, Peter teaches project management courses at Ryerson University, University of Toronto, University of Calgary, and Procept Associates Ltd.

Peter's career is built on over 40 years of project and leadership experience. Throughout his career, Peter has actively led projects and project managers in the areas of education, consulting, engineering, information technology health, and organizational change for multinational organizations. In a recent role, Peter successfully coached, mentored, and worked with project managers across six continents.

In prior roles, Peter managed portfolios of continuing education certificates (products) with over 4,000 enrollments, co-founded ZOOMtoLearn, and led programs of over 100 professionals and revenues over US$20 million per year implementing organizational change.

Over the past 20 years, Peter has taught almost 6,000 students in Project Management and Business Management in a variety of formats, including classroom, online, and intensive formats. Students in his classes come from a wide variety of industries, including financial, health care, government, non-profit, services, and entertainment. Peter's vast industry experience allows him to use examples to bring project management to life for all his students.

Peter has been an active volunteer with PMI for over 20 years. He served on the PMI Board of Directors for 6 years and was the Chair of the 2012 PMI Board. Also, Peter served on the PMI Educational Foundation Board of Directors, including being Chair of the 2018 PMIEF Board. Peter is a past president of the PMI Toronto Chapter and has served on several PMI Member Advisory Groups (MAGs).

In the Fall of 2007, Peter assumed the position of Chair of the Canadian Mirror Committee for the ISO PC236, which led to the development of ISO21500. Peter received his BSc (Engineering) from Queen's University and his MBA from the University of Toronto. He obtained his Project Management Professional (PMP)® credential in 1999, and in May 2008 he graduated from the PMI® Leadership Institute Master Class.

Dedication

To our lovely families, who gave us support and guidance throughout the journey, and unconditional love.

—Joanna Tivig and Peter Monkhouse

Table of Contents

List of Figures and Tables

Foreword

In this book, Joanna and Peter lead you to the new generation of product ownership. The product owner is a role that is independent of any particular approach to agility, such as the Scrum Framework or the Kanban Method. The product owner focuses on maximizing three important aspects of any business: delivering the most value for the money spent on product development, enabling fast time-to-market with frequent deliveries into the marketplace, and increasing customer satisfaction by incorporating fast feedback into the product development process.

My first experience with a good Product Owner occurred in 2005 at Capital One. I was coaching four Scrum teams, all working on a $20M program to migrate a data warehouse to a new technology platform. The Product Owner was a mid-level business manager who was responsible for the value delivered by the program. The Product Owner of these teams at Capital One was faced with a tough question at one point: should the delivery teams use temporary solutions to deliver high-value work every three weeks, or should they use permanent, but more complex solutions, that would only deliver value after an extended period of time (estimated to be 6 months or more). One of the most important parts of the product owner role is to empower the delivery teams to focus technical solutions on maximizing value. Not on minimizing cost.

The technical leads of the teams were convinced that the more complex permanent solutions were the right way to go. They put a lot of intellectual effort behind convincing the Product Owner to choose the complex permanent solution path. The technical leads argued that temporary solutions would cost more because the teams would have to revisit the solutions, possibly multiple times over the course of the program. Wisely, the Product Owner chose the path of delivering high value quickly. The teams changed their technical approach, and within just three months they had delivered a large proportion of the value of the program to the organization in the form of operational

cost reductions. At the time, I was deeply inspired by the Product Owner's focus on value delivery.

Since then, I have had the opportunity to coach numerous product owners at organizations of all sizes and in many industries. In my capacity as a Certified Scrum Trainer (TM) with Scrum Alliance, I have had the privilege of training over one thousand six hundred people in the basics of product ownership: product vision, understanding users and customers, measuring value, communicating with delivery teams, getting feedback from the marketplace, and understanding the mindset of agile product delivery. I have also worked myself as a product owner in several situations, including in my own business.

The product owner role is essential for business success with agility!

But not all of my experiences with product owners have been good.

It is easy for a person to be put into the role without sufficient preparation or support. Unfortunately, in many organizations, managers create crippled product teams: 'product owners' are often just business analysts responsible for writing all the user stories, teams do not actually ever see real customers from outside the organization, and rapid delivery into the marketplace is just a chimera obscured by bureaucratic red tape created by project management offices and compliance departments. Changing this situation is hard.

I believe that change starts with knowledge: when you have knowledge in the form of concepts, information, and skills, then you can, if you wish, start to make a difference. The key concepts to drive this change are value delivery, flow, and feedback. Every approach to business agility has practical techniques to implement these concepts. Joanna and Peter provide a wealth of knowledge in this book. That knowledge confirms and builds upon the basics of product ownership that you might get in a two-day training. And that knowledge helps you maximize value delivery, improve flow, and increase feedback.

—Mishkin Berteig

Preface

"The key to realizing a dream is to focus not on success but significance, and then even the small steps and little victories along your path will take on greater meaning."
—Oprah Winfrey

We have been instructors for the School of Continuing Studies at the University of Toronto for several years. When we were developing a course focused on leadership, we started talking about challenges organizations face today. Although we had very different life journeys, we immediately felt very strongly that the key to success for organizations are products and the value they deliver to customers. We began to work together and share our opinions on paper, which led to this book: *Gen P: New Generation of Product Owners Who Care About Customers.*

Working together felt like the right thing to do. In our journey, we began a joint collaboration, one being a workshop for the University of Toronto, Master of Management Analytics program, Rotman School of Management, followed by a product development workshop with Procter and Gamble. These events gave us confirmation that we were on our right track with the product topics and concepts explored in the book.

For Joanna, experiencing agile delivery for many years and working directly with product owners was the motivation to write the book. The inspiration came from a community of product owners willing to deliver value to customers but overseen by other roles or simply not considered important enough. Seeing organizations being more focused on profitability rather than value generation has been an element of interest and study. Why are organizations failing? What causes products to fade? Why agile and product development frameworks are still hard to grasp and implement? Because organizations need to realize that this is the time to try something else, and we are at the point where the old ways of working are obsolete. Product owners are the answer for the organizations to survive, therefore

growing a generation of product owners that are committed, knowledgeable, efficient and focused on value will show a new perspective.

In Peter's case, some time ago, his manager came to him and said, "Hey Peter you know about this project management thing, get yourself certified." At this point, he had been working on projects for years but did not realize he was a project manager. Peter discovered project management, got his PMP certification. As his career advanced, Peter got more interested in what happened to the product or services that his projects were creating. He realized that the products were being used to deliver benefits to customers and in some cases, these benefits helped customers achieve strategic objectives.

We went through our journey building a new product in the last couple of months. We validated our thinking and will continue to validate as we are launching our new product, this book. It is a journey of learning, experimentation and value delivery as we are already seeing feedback from customers and reviewers. How was this product built? Through care and protection, passion, pride, promotion and power, concepts referenced in our book. Hours of dedication for a product that is being launched from a simple idea, tested and experimented in various scenarios, a product that is intended to serve the needs of product owner communities. When we started this journey, we did not know whether the product would be successful or not, but we still built it, and we put all the effort into it.

This is it, new generation of product owners! Use everything you have, your passion, your pride, your care, your marketing, and leadership skills to build products that one day can and should be successful. Talking or complaining about it is not helping your cause. Doing it will give you the results you need and like in any iteration, learn from feedback and continue to build until customers appreciate your efforts and pay for them.

Acknowledgement

"No one who achieves success does so without acknowledging the help of others. The wise and confident acknowledge this help with gratitude."
—Alfred North Whitehead

We wish to thank the following people for their contribution to Gen P. Without their support and assistance, and we would not have been able to complete the book. It has been a great journey in which we acquired new friends and validated some great friendships but, most importantly, came together as a team.

We would like to thank our content reviewers: Lynn Shannon, Jamal El Ali, Sloba Glumac, and Steve Pereira, who provided extraordinary valuable comments, questions, and challenges that made us stay focused and committed. An extra thank you to Steve Pereira for his support on value stream mapping in Chapter 7.

A special thanks for Carole Smith for editing the book and finding our grammar errors, while aligning our writing styles.

Thank you to James Landers and Veena Balram, who provided real-life experiences, examples, and insights that have been used in the book.

For sure, this work would not exist, but for John Estrella's support and guidance in the process to write a book. His videos, focus sessions, and guidance have made a huge impact on our journey.

And of course, a big shout to Lyne Monkhouse, who found her inspiration on a Saturday morning and drew a colorful picture of what was to become the cover of the book.

We would like to acknowledge and thank those who have spent time to write books, articles, and blogs that we reference in the book, for

their dedication and sharing of their thoughts and knowledge with others.

Finally, we would like to acknowledge and thank anyone else who has taken the time to share their experiences with us, all of which helped us write Gen P and not yet mentioned.

INTRODUCTION

Gen P is about a new way for product owners to make their products grow and deliver value to loyal and potential customers. The product owner role is a simple but ambiguous role in most organizations. With the introduction of agile frameworks and particularly Scrum, product owners have started to be recognized as a role but limited to technology projects. However, product owners have existed in organizations for decades in one shape or another. They may have been in the marketing development, business analysis, client services or other parts of organizations. With the limited focus on product delivery, product owners have had minimal influence and chance for success.

Our goal in this book is to focus on how product owners can help organizations to be successful and in return what organizations can do for product owners. The book does not intend to override solutions offered by others, but to validate through continuous learning and experience that some solutions exist, and they can be implemented successfully. We believe many products are failing in the marketplace and some cases forcing organizations into bankruptcy because organizations are losing focus on product ownership. It is for the product owners to take what works best in the environment and apply their knowledge to see the results. Product owners who are more innovative and are able to sustain their products over long periods of time will transform industries and even change customer behaviors.

In this book, we draw our examples from organizations from a variety of sectors that have developed loyal customers and employees such as Disney, Airbnb, Netflix, Uber, Zappos, and many more. These examples provide real cases for success or experimentation that readers can learn from.

Gen P is envisioned to be a journey to success for the new generation of product owners. We start with challenges organizations face today such as increased diversity, disruptive technology, and changing business models. The challenges have solutions which we explore through skill builders and practical examples. The reader is given the opportunity to explore with ways of working that have roots in basic human behaviors, where primal instincts produce working habits focused on the need for survival and experiments to create valuable products. It is the new way of working, or a re-invented way meant to reduce waste and create value. These new ways will help crash the challenges to deliver strategy while building a product delivery culture. Culture and change play big roles in the productivity of teams and delivering outcomes for customers; therefore, we discuss how organizations can help themselves by embracing change and developing new mindsets.

We continue with an exploration into the life of a team delivering value to customers and what are the main ingredients for these performing teams. Introducing concepts like **SMART** teams and the power of efficiency, collaboration, value, and flow, the teams will achieve greater success. Next, we guide the reader to an in-depth analysis of iterations and productive experimentation methods. We start with prioritizations and estimates, dive into story mapping, and conclude with the power of MVP and break some strong myths about the MVP concept and show the reality of what is an enabler of productive releases.

The last part of the book is for the product owners to grasp the knowledge of ownership in different contexts with applied examples and tools to help in the journey of becoming the new generation of

product owners. What would be more important than having a circle of trust with the team to define the same purpose and work for the same goal, together as a unit that delivers value? Then as any good product owner would want is to, focus on the value delivery in a sustained way. Value stream maps are helping product owners and organizations identify faults and gaps in their processes and are becoming a productive way to maximize the potential of delivery chains. From there, we proceed in the space of continuous feedback from customers to improve a valuable product. Our idea about the product is that once launched, its life does not end, it just begins. Contrary to the idea of projects, products start to grow and mature the moment they are implemented, bringing more and more value to their customers.

The journey concludes with a focus on the new generation of product owners, their needs and expectations. To help product owners in their development and practice, we have identified key competencies that they can develop and apply in various scenarios. The focus is on the future, on the creative way to deliver value without the need for scaling, but with the need for sustainability. It is not about how many products you can develop, but how functional and desirable the products are. It is about how the products sell, how many returning customers organizations have and how they use customer feedback to build quality. In the end, this is the value-add for product owners to organizations and customers.

In this book, we take a broader perspective of product owners, not the narrow product owner role used for Agile projects. We believe that all organizations must have product owners for all their products whether they are external products selling to customers or internal products that are used to improve productivity and efficiency. Having product owners who are true owners of products, who listen to customers, and who use that feedback to continually improve products that deliver value to their customers, will ensure that the product continues to deliver value and the organization will continue to be successful.

There are product owners, and there are those that aspire to be product owners. This book is for both audiences guiding them to find valuable knowledge and inspirations for the products they need to deliver. For those who have a product mindset and are open to new ideas, who create value and build the long-lasting success of products, we want to offer you the challenge of joining the new generation of product owners: Gen P.

ABBREVIATIONS

ADKAR: a five-step model developed by Jeff Hiatt to guide individuals and organizations through change. The steps are awareness, desire, knowledge, ability, and reinforcement.

BCG: Boston Consulting Group.

CEO: Chief Executive Officer, in many cases, also the President, the most senior manager in the organization.

DVD: Digital versatile disc is a digital optical disc storage format invented in 1995 for storing audio, video and other digital files.

MVP: Minimum viable product, the minimum set of features included in a product that delivers value to a customer.

OKR: Objectives and Key Results, which was conceived at Intel but perfected at Google to ensure staff is focused on doing the right tasks.

PMI: Project Management Institute.

S&P 500: A stock market index that tracks the stocks of 500 large-cap U.S. companies.

SAP: Systems, Applications and Products is an Enterprise Resource Planning (ERP) system.

SVP: Senior Vice President.

SWOT: Strengths, weaknesses. opportunities, threats and can be used to analyze situations.

TPS: Toyota Production System which was developed by Toyota starting in the late 1940s through to the mid-1970s focusing on eliminating waste.

VUCA: Volatility, uncertainty, complexity, ambiguity introduced by Warren Bennis and Burt Nanus drawing on the leadership theories.

XP: Software development framework designed to improve the quality of the software and its ability to adapt to customer's changing needs.

CHAPTER

CHALLENGE THE STATUS QUO

*"Each year more than 30,000 new consumer products
are launched and 80% of them fail."*
–Clayton Christensen

Product owners, are you ready?

In 1975, Steven Sasson, a young engineer, invented the digital camera while working for Eastman Kodak. At the time, Kodak had a virtual monopoly on the United States photography market with an excellent business model where they made money on every step of the photographic process. Kodak's management reaction to Sasson's invention, as told by Sasson to the New York Times, was:

> *They were convinced that no one would ever want to look at their pictures on a television set. Print had been with us for over 100 years, no one was complaining about prints, they were very inexpensive, and so why would anyone want to look at their picture on a television set? (Estrin, 2015)*

In 1978, Kodak patented the digital camera and in 1989 Sasson and his colleague Robert Hills, invented the first modern digital single-lens-reflex camera while still working at Kodak. The management at Kodak was so focused on the film success that they missed the digital

revolution after inventing it. After all, how could Kodak make money without their main products of film, development services, paper, and chemicals? Kodak did not want to cannibalize its very successful photographic film business by introducing the disruptive technology of digital photography. Kodak did not realize that their current products were failing. To survive, Kodak should have evolved their current business model to take advantage of the new technology Sasson had invented.

On January 19, 2012, Kodak filed for Chapter 11 bankruptcy protection. In early 1997, Kodak's stock price was at its historical high of $94.75 and by January 19, 2012, it had dropped to $0.36. *(Estrin, 2015)*

Kodak was not ready.

Failing Products

Kodak is just one of many organizations that have failed, and there are others like Sears, Blockbuster, and Blackberry to name a few. It is not just organizations. Products are failing at an unprecedented rate. There are many studies that have been done showing a very high percentage of products fail *(Castellion, 2018; Emmer, 2018)*. The quote at the start of a chapter, from Clayton Christensen a professor at Harvard University, states that 80% of new consumer products fail *(Emmer, 2018)*. A Google search shows the percentage is as high as 95%. Inez Blackburn, a professor at the University of Toronto, says the failure rate of new grocery store products is 70% to 80%. Other studies, such as the Myths About New Product Failure Rates by George Castellion and Stephen K. Markham have shown that the actual failure rate is around 40% *(Castellion, 2018)*. Even at a 40% failure rate, this is still very high. The bottom line is that new products are most likely going to fail!

The effect of failing products reflects on an organization's struggle to succeed. Looking at the top 10 most valuable companies in 1997, twenty years later, only two of them—Microsoft and ExxonMobil—

are still in the top 10, even then ExxonMobil is barely hanging on in tenth place. It is interesting to note that Apple joined the top 10 list in 2010, Google in 2013, and Amazon in 2016 *(RankingTheWorld, 2019)*. Today more than ever, organizations are facing significant challenges that they must successfully overcome in order to survive.

What is causing organizations and products to struggle so much?

The U.S. Army Heritage and Education Center indicated that the United States Army War College introduced the term VUCA back in 1987 *(VUCA WORLD, 2019)*. VUCA stands for:

- **V**olatility. The dynamic nature of the environment today and the speed of exchange happens.
- **U**ncertainty. The lack of predictability and the prospects of surprises that are happening in the environment today.
- **C**omplexity. The multiple forces at play that impact customers.
- **A**mbiguity. The potential misreads or misunderstandings of signals received from customers and the environment.

The increase in volatility, uncertainty, complexity, and ambiguity means that you, as product owners, must seek new orientations and take a fresh approach to management and product delivery. Only then can you see positive results in changed situations. The VUCA world challenges the individual to seek new ways of doing things triggered by changes in the environment. You will need to understand the psychology and develop empathic behavior. In short, you need to be more concerned with humans and their needs *(VUCA WORLD, 2019)*.

Today, there are three forces that are dramatically changing the operating environment of organizations which cause volatility, uncertainty, complexity, and ambiguity.

The three forces are:

- **Diversity**. In today's global economy, competitors and cus-tomers come from all over the world. Your customers can go on the Internet and order products from anywhere and have the product delivered to their home in days. Anyone can also sell their products to customers anywhere in the world, inex-pensively, and with quick delivery. Diversity makes the con-sumer market very competitive. You are forced to think about how to deliver products globally to stay competitive on the market. When McDonald's expanded outside of the United States, they wanted to keep the same menu. But over time, McDonald's realized that they needed to allow for some flexibility to meet the tastes of different cultures. In the end, you can still buy a Big Mac wherever you go, as a signa-ture dish, just the flavors of the different components might be different (e.g., ketchup, pickles, or buns). Globalization forced McDonald's to change their product specifications to meet the needs of diverse global customers.

- **Technology**. Technology is changing all the time and at a more rapid pace. It is all about adapting technology to your business model. There are many examples of disruptive tech-nologies that are changing products and the way we live. In 1994, just two years after the Internet was invented, Jeff Be-zos founded Amazon. A year later, Amazon began selling books online competing with local booksellers. Over the years, Amazon expanded online products and was competing against the traditional brick and mortar retailers. By 2018, those traditional retailers were struggling, including Sears who filed for Chapter 11 bankruptcy protection on October 15, 2018. Technology is creating significant challenges for or-ganizations as they try to figure out what their competitors are doing and which opportunities the new technologies pre-sent to create more value to their customers.

- **Business models.** Competition is forcing organizations to change their business models. Competition comes from places that you never thought would be possible, and it is no longer the store around the corner. Disruptive technology leads to new business models, such as Uber creating an application that matches people that want rides to those willing to provide rides. This application started to compete with the taxicab industry. New business models are creating more competition. Zappos has been created on a loyalty and relationship marketing business model that used the organization's people and resources to work towards establishing and increasing customer and stakeholder loyalty. The chain of events in this model includes a good quality product and excellent service that creates customer satisfaction. This leads to loyalty of repeat customers and results in profitability. Zappos has been successful in its goals as about 75% of the business comes from repeat buyers. Did traditional shoe stores ever think that their customers would buy shoes online? No. In fact, Tony Hsieh, the founder of Zappos initially got his shoes from retail stores to fulfill his orders *(Bulygo, 2019)*.

Figure 1.1: Forces Impacting Product Delivery

The result of diversity, technology, and business models creates a much more global and complex environment for the organization and its products. No wonder over 40% of new products are failing the first few years.

Why is all the disruption happening?

This disruption has three systemic causes. The first is outlined in the book *Age of Discovery: Navigating the Storms of the New Renaissance* by Ian Goldin and Chris Catana *(Golden, 2016)*. The authors argue that the invention of the Internet in 1992 is the most dramatic change since the invention of the Gutenberg printing press in the mid-1400s. The Internet has made such a dramatic change in how information is processed, gathered, accessed, and distributed which has never been experienced since the invention of the Gutenberg printing press. The Internet changes the way people think, act and by extension the way people consume products. The printing press had large societal changes leading to the renaissance of the 1500s. Just as the smartphone, made possible by the internet, is changing society today.

The second cause is the impact of the Industrial Age on how society has moved over the last three hundred years from Industry 1.0 to 4.0. The focus of Industry 1.0 and 2.0 was on scalability, creating manufacturing plants to mass-produce products and meet growing customer demands. Later into Industry 3.0 and now Industry 4.0, technology has taken over the repetitive jobs in order to allow organizations to be more efficient by replacing the staff hired in Industry 1.0. The changes in Industry 4.0 are even more extensive with the recognition of networking and the 'Internet of Things'. Devices have never been more connected. Data is being collected at an unprecedented rate from everywhere. You now have more access to information about who is buying your products and how your customers are using their products. As product owners, you now have more information about how the teams are performing and how the supply chain works. With all of this information, organizations are figuring out new ways of doing things, which is creating Industry 4.0 *(Howard, 2018)*.

During the ages of Industry 1.0 to Industry 2.0, the focus was on training humans to be able to repeat tasks in a consistent way. In Industry 3.0, the repetitive tasks done by humans were replaced by robots. With Industry 4.0, humans need different skills to focus on creativity, problem-solving, and innovation that are currently hard to automate.

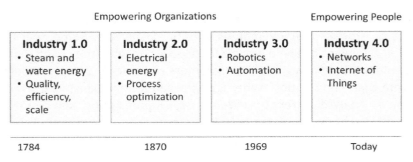

Figure 1.2: Direction of Industry

The third cause is the four-generation workforce: Baby boomers, Gen X, Millennials (Gen Y) and Gen Z. In recent years, there has been a dramatic change in the composition of the workforce. The aging baby boomers are working until they are much older, while Gen Z is now entering the workforce. Studies show that each generation is marked by significant events that happen in their youth, such as the assassination of President Kennedy in 1963 for the baby boomers and September 11, 2001, for Millennials. The differences in the generations are impacting how organizations are structured and get work done. In addition, the customers are segmented in similar ways and add to the uncertainty and complexity of business plans.

The result is many organizations are not able to successfully launch new products. Failure costs money and time, which organizations no longer have. Product owners need to find mechanisms to be able to deliver new products quickly, that their customers value and be able to deal with complexity and diversity. And, all of this has to be done while reacting to the changing technology and changing needs. The new generation of product owners must be able to overcome the three forces of diversity, technology, and business model.

Strategy Yes, Delivery No

"A brilliant strategy, blockbuster product, or breakthrough technology can put you on the competitive map, but only solid execution can keep you there" *(Neilson, 2015)*. Over the past years, there has been a lot of work done in the consulting space to help organizations create a strategy that overcomes specific challenges. Some specific methodologies can help organizations focus on what they need to do to meet the demands of their customers while dealing with pressure from their competition. Whether an organization uses Porter's Five Forces analysis, Strengths, Weakness, Opportunities, and Threats (SWOT) analysis, Playing to Win, Blue Ocean Strategy, Scenario Thinking, or any other approach, they all guide organizations in deciding what their mission and vision are and what key strategic objectives they need in order to be successful.

Having a strategy is one thing; being able to deliver the strategy is something else. Employees at three out of every five companies rated their organization weak at execution. When asked if they agreed with the statement "Important strategic and operational decisions are quickly translated into action," the majority answered no *(Neilson, 2015)*. Research done by the Project Management Institute (PMI) Brightline initiative has found that only one in ten organizations can deliver their strategies successfully. If organizations want to be successful, they must develop a good strategy, and they must be able to execute it.

To successfully deliver strategy, organizations have to overcome five key challenges:

- **Culture**. Michael Porter's famous quote is *"Culture eats strategy for breakfast,"* has started to resonate with top management over the last ten years. Culture is about how things are really getting done in the organization. If you have developed a strategy and you are unable to change the culture, the strategy will not be successful. The culture will override the

new strategy, and the staff will just keep doing what they always have done.

- **Structure**. Typically, the structure of an organization is set up for optimal delivery of products and services. For an organization to deliver a new strategy, its structure needs to change to support the delivery of new products. This is not just a change to the hierarchy, it also includes changing capabilities, policies, procedures, processes, and other existing systems in the organization to allow the strategy to be implemented.

- **Focus**. To be successful in strategy delivery, product owners have to stay focused on the strategic goals of the organization. However, if there are new leadership and new ideas in the organization, or new products from competitors and new requests from customers, all of these can distract product owners from delivering their products according to the strategy. In this age of rapid change, this will lead to failure.

- **Execution**. When done correctly, strategy execution is a disciplined process, a logical set of connected activities done by an organization for a common purpose. To achieve strategic objectives, organizations need to develop products that have benefits and create value for customers. To create products, product owners must use feedback to create iterations that deliver the highest priority value to customers.

- **Change**. An organization should have a strategy that focuses on delivering sustained value to its customers. Bad assumptions, missed signals in the ever-changing environment, unexpected technology disruptors, and poor decision making can result in misalignment between strategy and customer value. Organizations need to ensure they adapt their strategy to reflect the changing customer needs.

Figure 1.3: Challenges of Strategy Delivery

Strategy delivery is a notorious and perennial challenge. On top of everything else, the ability to make decisions quickly and act in situations of crisis will make or break the strategy. Even at 'resilient organizations', only two-thirds of employees agree that important strategic and operational decisions are quickly translated into actions. If organizations continue to attack their delivery problems with only structural or motivational initiatives, they will continue to fail.

Take Your Product on a Journey

The Boston Consulting Group (BCG) has popularized the product life cycle with four quadrants: question marks, stars, cash cows, and dogs *(Hanlon, 2019)*.

This is the traditional product life cycle where products will start with an introduction stage as a question mark or simply an idea. It is not known if the product is going to be successful or not. If the product does not show a chance for success, it is dropped at this stage. The products that show signs of being successful move to the next stage, growth.

In the growth stage, the product is attracting more customers and achieving a higher market share. When the growth has reached maturity, products are called cash cows. The idea in the cash cow stage is to optimize the delivery of the product to allow for the maximization of profit. Inevitably, the product's revenue starts to slow down due to changing technology, fashion, or demographics and the product moves into the decline stage and is called dogs. In this stage, an exit strategy for the product is used. In some cases, products can be re-invented to extend their productive life.

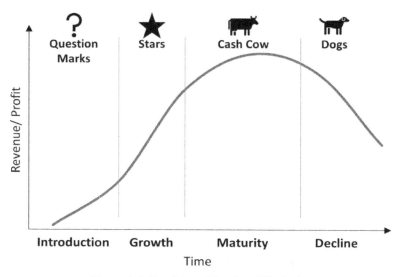

Figure 1.4: Traditional Product Life Cycle

The traditional product life cycle was fine back in the 1970s and 1980s, and even until the 1990s. The challenges of diversity, technology, and business models are forcing product life cycles to change and adapt. In general, the idea of having an introduction, growth, maturity, and decline phase for product life cycle works. The problems are with the time it takes for a product to go through the introduction and growth phases and the lack of investment in the maturity phase of the product.

In today's world, the agile product life cycle can be used to get a product to market quickly and extend its life. The agile product life cycle consists of three main phases: customer problem, market validation, and agile execution. The first phase involves identifying the customer problem and possible products to their problem. Organizations then need to decide which possible product delivers the most value to their target customers and quickly determine if it is going to be successful or not. To do this, in the market validation phase, organizations can adopt an approach of identifying a minimum viable product (MVP) that can be launched quickly and obtain feedback from the customer. Then, using iteration in the agile execution phase, products are enhanced and changed in growth and maturity phases by adding features to deliver more and more value to customers.

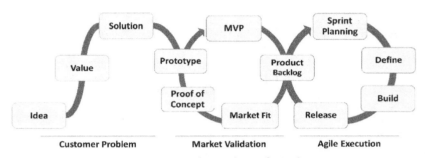

Figure 1.5: Agile Product Life Cycle

The MVP is defined by Eric Ries *(Agile Alliance, 2019) "as that version of a new product which allows a team to collect the maximum amount of validated learning about customers with the least effort."* Adding features that are based on customer feedback, changes in technology, reaction of competitors and other changes in the environment will extend the product's life.

In the traditional product life cycle, the product is very well defined with as many features as possible in the introduction stage before moving to the growth stage. In contrast, with the agile product life cycle, the minimum features are gathered first, and more features are continuously added to the product throughout all stages of the product life cycle to extend and expand the product. This allows for

the product to evolve and adjust to the changes in technology, competitors' reactions and most importantly to feedback from customers.

For Zappos, the differentiating factor has been a concentrated focus on the best customer service that can be offered for an online business. The company continues to offer free domestic shipping on all orders with no minimum order amount or any other caveats. In addition, they continue to offer free and hassle-free returns for their customers. This takes away any apprehension a customer may have about making a shoe or clothing purchase online without being able to try on or feel the product. Tony Hsieh *(Bulygo, 2019)*, the founder and CEO of Zappos wrote: *"If we're serious about building our brand to be about the very best customer service and customer experience; then customer service shouldn't just be a department—it should be the entire company."* For Zappos, Tony Hsieh identified the MVP, a website with pictures of a few shoes that he could buy from a local shoe store. Then, based on feedback from customers, he continuously enhanced his product by adding features that have increased customer loyalty for over 20 years!

With the constant monitoring of the product, the new generation of product owners can identify when the product is no longer delivering value and minimize the time a product spends in the decline phase, thus reducing waste on trying to save a product that is struggling. By not supporting struggling products, product owners can free up people and money to work on new products that will support your organization's strategy.

Using the agile product life cycle to create the MVP and continuing to enhance the product based on customer feedback will allow you to:
- Release your product to the market in the shortest time;
- Reduce implementation costs;
- Test the demand for your product before releasing a full-fledged product;
- Avoid failures and large capital losses;

- Gain valuable insight into what works and what doesn't work;
- Work directly with your clients and analyze their behaviors and preferences; and
- Gather and enhance your user base *(Tokareva, 2018).*

The new generation of product owners needs to be able to define the MVP for their product development and then iterate to continuously add value to their products.

ACHIEVE

Are you ready?

As a product owner are you asking these questions:
- What are you doing in your organization to make sure your products are thriving?
- Are you using an agile product life cycle?
- Are you creating your MVP and incrementally adding value?
- Are you focusing on execution?
- Are you focused on empowerment to drive the success of your product?

The new generation of product owners must!

In the Scrum Framework, especially in the software development sector, a product owner is the single person who is responsible for the success of a product and for maximizing the value of that product *(Scrum.org).* In other sectors, the role of the product owner or product manager is used to support products at various points in the traditional product life cycle. For organizations to address the challenges of diversity, technology, and business model, the role of the product owner must change and evolve. There is a new generation of product owners, and they belong in all sectors.

The new generation of product owners owns their products. Product ownership means that there will be stewardship of the product throughout the product life cycle ensuring that you are producing products that are valued by customers while minimizing waste. Every product in an organization, in any sector, must have a product owner with the accountability of determining the features to be added or removed from the product, to ensure that the product will deliver value and delight the customer, and be able to solve problems for customers.

Here is a real-life example of an organization transforming to a product owner structure to protect its equipment used to manufacture products from cyberattacks.

Jim is an executive with a global medical equipment manufacturer. Jim's department is in charge of cybersecurity to ensure that there are no cyberattacks on any of the equipment worldwide. To do this, Jim has divided his group into four teams each focused on a product line, with a dedicated product owner who is responsible to ensure that each piece of equipment is protected from a cyberattack. Jim empowered the product owners to take ownership of their product lines with full accountability and decision-making powers. He expects the product owners to prioritize the feedback from stakeholders ranging from the operators of the equipment, the researchers who identify potential cyber risks, the organization's risk group who identify potential threats, and others to ensure that the most critical updates are completed. The updates have to be done quickly to all equipment. In the case of cybersecurity, all it takes is one piece of equipment that has not been updated and an attack can be a success, putting the whole organization at risk. This means the product owners need to collaborate to implement the updates. The product owners also need to ensure that the team has the skills, resources, and budget to do the work that is required. The product owners must understand the process involved to develop the proper updates that stop possible cyberattacks.

By putting the product owners in place, Jim's department has successfully stopped any cyberattacks on the equipment in the organization. The product owners are also positioned to look out for additional features of their products ensuring the delivery of value for years to come.

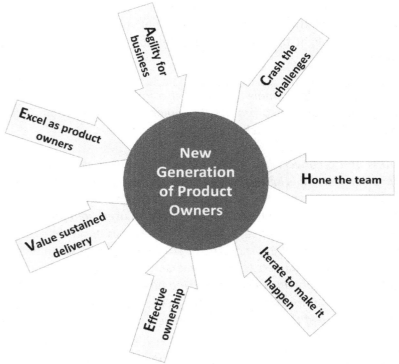

Figure 1.6: ACHIEVE Product Ownership

Throughout the next seven chapters in this book, we will go through the seven key areas where organizations and individuals need to **ACHIEVE** product ownership.

These are:

- **A**gility for business. Use agile concepts to reduce time and waste in producing products.
- **C**rash the challenges. Find solutions and quickly make decisions on the plans of action.

42

- **H**one the team. Align the team to the needs of the customer and ultimately, the product.
- **I**terate to make it happen. Learn and improve through cycles of continuous delivery to obtain customer feedback quickly.
- **E**ffective ownership. Nurture, protect and focus on the product to maintain its accuracy and desirability
- **V**alue sustained delivery. Develop value models through assessments in the right market segment.
- **E**xcel as product owners. Continuously grow the skills to bring new ideas to product management.

ACHIEVE will guide you to join the new generation of product owners that build best-in-class products. As a product owner, you need to demonstrate that you have something different to offer; something that will provide superior value, a product that shows you care about your customers.

AGILITY FOR BUSINESS

"If you can't explain it simply,
you don't understand it well enough."
–Albert Einstein

In the early 1990s, as computers began to proliferate in organizations, software development faced a crisis. At the time, it was widely referred to as 'the application development crisis', or 'application delivery lag'. Industry experts estimated that the time between a validated business need and an actual application in production was about three years. For those products with a software development component, such as phone switches, automobiles, or aircraft, the software was often an afterthought, mostly because software development did not start until the hardware design was fixed. But building the software just was not a priority for most teams at the time *(Varhol, 2019)*.

In the Beginning …

In 1994, The Standish Group published its first CHAOS Report. The report documents that *"… a staggering 31.1% of projects will be canceled before they ever get in chaos. Further results indicate 52.7% of projects will cost 189% of their original estimates."* The report goes on to estimate *"… that in 1995 American companies and government*

agencies will spend $81 billion for canceled software projects." The report concludes that *"... the average is only 16.2% for software projects that are completed on-time and on-board"* *(The Standish Group, 1994).*

The frustrations felt by both technology executives and software professionals, led to the Snowbird meeting in Utah in early 2001 when a group of developers got together to discuss the growing field of what used to be called lightweight methods, later renamed agile methods. At that meeting, the terms 'light' and 'lightweight' were more commonly used rather than 'agile' or 'agility', although none of the participants were particularly satisfied with that description. The result of the meeting was the development of the Agile Manifesto and the twelve Agile Principles. *(Varhol, 2019).*

Rapid feedback and willingness to change turned out to be the key features of the agile movement. If the software team is not confident in understanding what the user needs, it delivers a first approximation and then listens to feedback. Agile processes are a necessary first step in fast customer feedback, but continuous delivery requires even more radical change. It means that product owners and teams iterate based on their best knowledge at the time yet are fully prepared to remove or change features immediately based on customer reactions.

The fundamental point about agility is the ease of doing things. It is not about speed or flexibility as much as it is about the natural way of doing something you like to do. Doing things with ease is possible when people feel comfortable and confident about them, they feel more creative, more artistic, and they develop and change fast. On the other hand, an agile mindset welcomes, and embraces change and is not upset with any change that is presented, whether in a crisis situation or not. You easily adapt and get excited when something new and unusual is presented to you. Whether you have to perform the same old task that you have done hundreds of times before or something totally new that you have never done before, you welcome it and find a way to make it pleasurable.

You see boredom and irritation as an opportunity to automate or innovate and fear or overwhelm as a challenge to grow. As a situation of crisis occurs, it seems like the perfect situation to innovate. That is why organizations remain in the status quo until something in their routine triggers a change, such as obsolete technology, competition, customer demands or regulations. An agile mind stops and asks what the goal of the task is before jumping in and doing it.

To understand why the agile mindset is key to product ownership, it needs a deeper look into how our minds work. The human brain is programmed since youth to function in a certain way, and it requires practice and training to change it. That is why people have two parts of the brain. One is more pragmatic, logical, and prefers order while the other is more creative, focused on the passion and the courage to achieve more. As people work on certain tasks, they would know exactly which part of our brain to use and why they excel at some activities and not at others. As they grow their minds and they have more experience, some parts of the brain grow with them, depending on how often they put these parts to work.

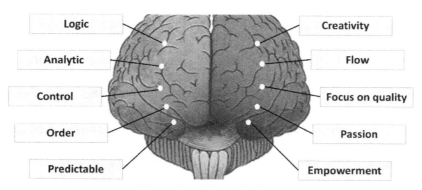

Figure 2.1: The Agile Brain

According to the growth mindset theory, a concept that is often discussed these days, the people that are open to new situations are more likely to survive in critical situations *(Dames, 2016)*. The people with a fixed mindset, are not open to any new situations, and they

47

prefer routine as a safe way of living. The brain helps people in their journey to deliver results, so here is how the principles of execution are divided between the two hemispheres.

Agility uses primarily the right side of the brain, where human behaviors and creativity are more prominent. The left side is about logical tasks, frameworks, and practices, also called 'doing agile', while the right side is about emotional and social aspects of work, transparency, and collaboration, values, and principles, also called 'being agile'. That is the reason why agile mindset teams seem to be more flowing, focused on interactions, relationships and trust between team members. They let their creativity and courage dominate and have passion as the main driver for success. This part of the brain also helps product owners define the features customers will desire. Most everything on the right side will make product owners successful, while the left side will help them prioritize and predict what customers need. Managing the parts of your brain and calling the ones that will help you do the job will become part of a mastered routine.

The question is, how can you transform the situations you have not encountered before in logical patterns. The concept of 'keeping an open mind' or 'looking at the big picture' is referenced more and more in the workplace, encouraging everyone to absorb everything that comes to them and make the best out of every situation. As change is in everything people do, learning new things represents a challenge to a brain that likes routine. People have the tendency to close their minds to everything that comes at them as difficult or new. This puts people and organizations in a 'freeze' state. When the 'freeze' state happens, people need to rely more on their right side of the brain and encourage it to explore the changes in their lives. The more they train their brain to open, and to use the right side, the easier it will be for them to do everything they are confronted to do on a daily basis.

With a basic understanding of the brain, here are the similarities between the agile principles that were written in the Agile Manifesto in 2001 and the product owner's basic way of thinking.

Agile Principle	What it means for the Product Owner
Our highest priority is to satisfy the customer through early and continuous delivery of valuable software.	Customer satisfaction and desirability are the bread and butter of the product owner; making the customer buy the products offered and making the customer want to buy more is the main responsibility of this role.
Welcome changing requirements, even late in development. Agile processes harness change for the customer's competitive advantage.	Any product owner would love to have the ability to change priorities as the product development progresses; this is an enabler for product owners to reasonably add or decrease the scope to make the product more sellable.
Deliver working software frequently, from a couple of weeks to a couple of months, with a preference to the shorter timescale.	Performance and quality make or break products; product owners care that their products work in the hand of the customers and new features are introduced as frequent and as seamless as possible; this is for all products, not just software.
Business people and developers must work together daily throughout the project.	The ultimate business technology quarrel must end! Product owners, administrators, and specialists must work together for the sake of the products and the customer using it.
Build projects around motivated individuals. Give them the environment and support they need and trust them to get the job done.	The dynamics of the team are fundamental for the successful launch of a product. Product owners, together with scrum masters, flow masters, or project managers, keep the team motivated and focused on priorities.
The most efficient and effective method of conveying information to and within a development team is a face-to-face conversation.	Product owners are part of the working team, sitting very close to the team and making quick decisions, so the team is not stalled.
Working software is the primary measure of progress.	Product owners are visual people, and they like to see everything that they envisioned in their requirements: a working product will prove the product owner's thinking.
Agile processes promote sustainable development. The sponsors, developers, and users should be able to maintain a constant pace indefinitely.	Maintaining a backlog that supports and feeds features to the working team is the main priority order. To deliver increased value to customers is the key responsibility of the product owner.
Continuous attention to technical excellence and good design enhances agility.	A well-designed product that is reliable for the customer to use at anytime, anywhere is fundamental for customer satisfaction and delivers value.
Simplicity—the art of maximizing the amount of work not done—is essential.	Eliminating waste and requirements that customers do not need should be the main focus of product owners.
The best architectures, requirements, and designs emerge from self-organizing teams.	The team is accountable or responsible for doing their work and for self-organizing when necessary.
At regular intervals, the team reflects on how to become more effective, then tunes and adjusts its behavior accordingly.	Reflections and retrospectives are part of the Sprint events, and they are done in coordination with the team.

Table 2.1: Agile Principles

Ease of doing things lead to improved proficiency which in turn becomes higher productivity. Productive people spend less time doing things because everything comes naturally to them, using learning habits, and learning as much as possible while they produce results. Productive people will not necessarily do the same thing the same way, on the contrary, they will try to improve the process and do things better every time. The routine in what they do only seems routine because it is done faster and much easier.

Going back to basics, by using their right side of the brain, product owners are able to encourage creativity and innovation to generate value for the business and customers. With the help of Agile Manifesto principles, product owners can focus on five major themes:

1. Customer experience
2. Fast and simple deliveries
3. Great teams
4. Continuous improvement
5. Change management

The emphasis in these five themes is on eliminating as much waste as possible and focusing on the customer. These themes are the basics for the product owner and represent the critical core of success. In order to stay in business, you need to have a customer who likes your products, a delivery pipeline that delivers these products fast and in great shape with continuous improvement, a great team to make all of this happen, and a process to deal with any changes that come your way.

The Customer Says

It is no coincidence that the first Agile Manifesto principle is about customer experience. Gone are the times when customers will buy anything offered to them. So much for Henry Ford's quote from 1909, *"You can have any color you want as long as it is black."* If a customer didn't like something they were offered, the product owner could say: We hear you, but that's what we have', or 'We will consider your

request' and leave it at that. In today's competitive market, customers are more selective, they have access to information and comparison methods, plus the diversity of products has been visible in the last few years. U.S. consumer-goods companies, for example, increased the number of new products introduced annually by nearly 60 percent from 2002 through 2011, resulting in significantly higher costs throughout their supply chains. However, those companies' total sales during that period grew at just 2.8 percent per year, a rate that only slightly exceeded inflation. A similar disparity between the number of products launched and the revenue growth achieved has occurred in Europe, across industries *(Pichlar, 2014)*. Competition has created a world where the customer rules. Feedback from customers on their experience with a product has become fundamental to measure product success. Product owners listen to what customers say about their products because both noise and good feedback make our products grow while increasing the organization's market share.

Andrea, a high school student who was upset with the service she received in a shoe store, did what teenagers do and wrote on the store's Facebook page about the experience. Within 20 minutes after the posting, not only did Andrea receive a public apology from the store, but she was invited to connect with the store manager and arrange for an appropriate discount that would compensate for the bad experience. What would have happened if the shoe store had not replied so quickly and positively to Andrea's post?

The key to effective customer experience is listening. For product owners, it is important to consider three sides of listening in customer engagement: **relate**, **reflect**, and **reshape**. If you as a product owner manage to do these 3Rs of customer listening properly, you will be very successful in managing customer interactions.

- **Relate**. Relating to what customers are saying about your product means that you can understand the pains and gains and make educated decisions about the actions you may take.

51

- **Reflect**. Reflecting on what customers are saying, without fear of negative feedback about your product means that you are thinking about a plan of action and make the best decisions going forward on behalf of the customer.

- **Reshape**. Reshaping the way you approach the product going forward, while making sure that you would make continuous changes to the product, to keep the customers happy.

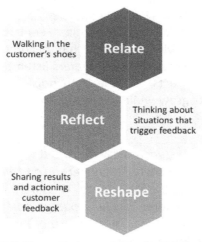

Figure 2.2: Three Customer Listening Methods (3Rs)

To the surprise of organizations, the customer has become the boss. Diversity and technology, especially the internet, have provided customers with reliable information about choices, as well as the innovative ability to connect with other customers. Suddenly the customer expects immediate, customized value. The voice of the customer has become the first voice organizations have learned to listen to and deprioritize all the other voices in the process.

'Relate' means to receive the best feedback from your customers and be able to put yourself in your customer's shoes. By doing this, product owners can create situations for discussions using multiple chan-

nels. Channels can range from digital applications to customer contact centers, to drop off boxes, whatever makes it easier for the customer. The second step is to filter all unnecessary distractions. This means removing barriers such as technology or confirmation biases, so they can provide clear feedback without being biased by situations that are happening with your product.

In reflecting, you need to review the feedback you have received and determine an action plan to address the feedback. To do this, product owners should filter and categorize the feedback to allow you to identify areas of focus. If you are not sure what the customer is saying, do not hesitate to go back to the customer and ask for clarification. The actions you develop must be designed to enhance the value to the customer.

'Reshape' means product owners share the results of the feedback to the customers and the actions you are planning to take with the customer. This last step is key as it shows the customer that their input is valued, and you want to improve to exceed their expectations.

Sarah is a Product Owner and is launching an online course. She needs to build an online site for potential students to come and register for the courses they want to take. After a few weeks, she wants to get feedback on the experience they had in registering for courses. The first R is 'relate', to create a situation where people who use the site can provide feedback quickly and easily. They can either go to the contact us link or have a separate window on the screen where they can provide feedback using 5-star methods. The next R is 'reflect', where Sarah should look at the feedback that was provided and filter the unnecessary distractions. This is especially the case if there are glitches in the system. If Sarah needs more clarification on the feedback, she ensures that there is a way to go back to the user to ask for more information to allow her to make the experience better. After the feedback has been clarified, Sarah compiles and analyzes it to ensure it is consistent. Then action plans to address the issues raised should be developed. The last thing Sarah does is to 'reshape' the

feedback in a format that she can share with the people using the registration site.

In this example, Sarah had a difficult challenge of testing features that were referenced in customer feedback and had to be replicated. She had to develop and test multiple scenarios in order to obtain the results in the feedback. She responded to every customer feedback, thanking them for the feedback and giving them details on how the complaints are being resolved, or just thanking customers for the positive feedback.

Feedback from Customers	Actions
"Payment process is very difficult, and address did not auto-populate."	Test payment system; introduce a business rule to auto-populate button
"The next step button did not work; had to try again."	Test "next step" button links; make changes to ensure appropriate links
"The system is fantastic; it is much easier than the previous registration site."	Do nothing; maintain same level of satisfaction

Table 2.2: Customer Feedback Example

Listening to customers is not an easy task, the 3Rs will help you focus your attention and interactions with customers on important topics: understanding the feedback, reviewing the feedback and sharing the feedback results back to your customer. The end goal is to use feedback to build better products and continuously satisfy your customer's needs.

From Waste to Success

The tenth principle of the Agile Manifesto is *"Simplicity—the art of maximizing the amount of work not done—is essential."* Equally in Lean, one of the five principles is mapping the value stream, where the goal is to show the steps that do not create value and then find ways to eliminate those wasteful steps. Waste can be defined as cost less value. If the costs are higher than the value of the outcomes produced, then the waste is higher. It means that there will always be a

waste if product owners are not able to produce value for the features customers pay for. One of the reasons for waste is multitasking. It costs organizations much more than the value people produce while multitasking.

Waste = Cost - Value

Figure 2.3: Waste Formula

It is Monday morning and Mary starts working on updating content on the newly launched website based on feedback from customers. Over the weekend, there was a report of a pricing error that must be corrected quickly. She estimates it will take approximately 30 minutes to do the update. She has other things to do immediately after the website is updated, including updating a product backlog that will take 30 minutes. Mary settles down to work on the update by first locating where the error is. She finds the webpage with the error in ten minutes and then the phone rings, her boss is calling. Mary has to stop work on the update to talk to her boss. The call only takes five minutes, but Mary's boss wants a copy of a presentation Mary did two weeks ago immediately. It takes Mary another five minutes to find the presentation and to email it to her boss. Mary can now return to updating the website. However, she is still thinking about the presentation and the experience. It was not a good experience which makes it harder to focus on updating the website. Finally, after 30 minutes of the phone call from her boss, Mary continues her work on the website. It takes Mary ten minutes to find the web page and just when she finds the page, one of her colleagues, who sits beside Mary, comes and asks for her opinion on one of the projects she is working on. Mary knows this is a very complex project with challenging stakeholders. Mary and her colleague talk about various scenarios to address the situation that Mary's colleague is facing. After 30 minutes, Mary's colleague has a path forward, and Mary was happy to help. Mary returns to the web page, now what was the problem? Then one of her colleagues suggests it is time to go for a quick coffee. It was quick; 10 minutes later Mary is back to finish updating the web page.

Let us review Mary's morning so far. Mary has been at work for 100 minutes. During that time, she has worked for 20 minutes on her number one priority, and the web page is still not updated. In Mary's first 100 minutes of work (the cost), she worked 20 minutes on your top priority (the value). The waste is 80 minutes.

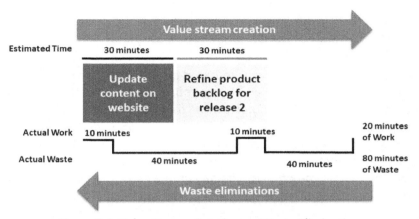

Figure 2.4: Value Stream Creation vs. Waste Elimination

This is happening every day, not only in projects and teams but in offices in every organization that believes multitasking is a productive way of working. The waste in product management is similar. We introduced the traditional product life cycle in Chapter 1. To launch a product, the product owner would talk to customers and other stakeholders to gather as many requirements as possible. The product owner would then review the requirements, prioritize them, and develop the scope for the product. A team is then formed to deliver the scope. Of course, as the team estimates the work and starts the development of the product, the customer informs you of a regulation change which—if not implemented—means the product cannot be launched. As a product owner, you do not want to disrupt the team and the work that has been developed. If you do, then the team will lose focus, and the product will be delayed, just like Mary's Monday morning. However, if you do not change the product scope, the customer will not receive the value as the product cannot be launched.

When it comes to improving business processes and eliminating waste, lean process improvement is the solution. Traditionally lean business processes have emerged in the manufacturing sector and go way back to Henry Ford. Ford consistently mapped and moved around parts of standard work to create what he called flow production. This was perceived as a revolutionary step from the practices of Taylor's scientific management. But although Ford managed to create flow on the assembly line, he could not obtain variety at the start of making cars. For example, the first car Ford produced on the assembly line, the Model T, was only available in one color, black. In the 1930s, Toyota revisited Ford's original thinking and mapped the product with the processes, creating Toyota Production System (TPS). At the top of the model, they put the different products, and on the left, they mapped the processes. The more standardized the processes, the easier it will be to produce large quantities of products. The continuous flow process makes the product endure different operations of the same automated product line so that all products are manufactured with very similar characteristics *(Staples, 2018)*.

Since the 1930s, continued research and practice have developed the following principles:

- **Improve Quality**. Mary would build a better document if she could maintain her focus on the task. Being connected and disconnected from the task various times causes her to lose focus and miss valuable information in her deck.

- **Eliminate Waste**. Mary can eliminate wasteful activities by empowering her direct reports to make decisions and research for further information and solution with the teams. Mary can also provide her insights during team meetings.

- **Reduce Lead Time**. While avoiding the interruptions is the best way to avoid lead times, Mary can also reduce the gap between the conversation with her direct report and going back to her slide by making high-level notes before she starts

building her deck. This way, she can remember the key points she wanted the make.

- **Reduce Total Costs**. Mary needs to reduce the indirect costs, in this case, the two interruptions, so that she can increase the value she produces by putting together a valuable presentation that she can take to the management team.

Lean thinking provides general guidelines to improve any product or service delivery through the productivity and scalability of the business. The reduction of waste is crucial when you reduce the people and processes required for an activity. They can be utilized elsewhere to support your organization in achieving its strategic goals.

Keep it Simple

The butterfly effect is the idea that small things can have non-linear impacts on a complex system. The concept is imagined with a butterfly flapping its wings and causing a typhoon. Of course, a single act like the butterfly flapping its wings cannot cause a typhoon. Small events can, however, serve as catalysts that act on starting conditions. Complexity is used as a catch-all for things that are not simple or not intuitive. Complexity should not be restricted to technology. Being complex is different from being complicated *(McChrystal, 2015)*. An iPhone X, if opened, would look complicated, with the multiple little shiny parts, but those parts are joined one to the next in a relatively simple way.

Complexity, however, occurs when the number of interactions between components increases dramatically. The interdependencies between communication networks allow for viruses to spread quickly. This is where things become quickly unpredictable. The point would be not to try to predict everything through leveraging outcomes. As McChrystal points out the term 'butterfly effect' is almost always misused. It has become synonymous with 'leverage'—the idea of a small thing that has a big impact, with the implication that, like a lever, it can be manipulated to the desired end. This misses the point of Lorenz's insight on the butterfly effect. The reality is those

small things in a complex system may have no effect or a massive one, and it is almost impossible to know which will be the case.

Because of the multitude of interactions, complex systems allow non-linear change, meaning that a change can occur anywhere in a system without triggering any logical sequence. These types of unpredictable situations make us very uncomfortable. Not knowing how our customers will react to having a new feature on their mobile applications makes product owners feel very nervous. Imagine how anyone feels when a complex core system breaks, and nobody knows what caused it. The advancement of technology over the last two or three decades has contributed to complexity and has left many managers struggle with the pace of change they were exposed to.

Taylor's scientific management was designed for complicated problems, rather than complex ones, with the result, the MBA courses from the 1980s have become suddenly obsolete. Companies realized that they are steadily finding their way to failure or success depending on the speed of dealing with change.

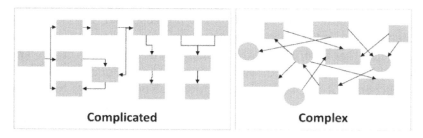

Complicated   Complex

Figure 2.5: Complicated and Complex Systems

Working with complex systems is not an easy task. Processes can be used to simplify systems and allow for speed in delivery. Complexity can, therefore, be decomposed into simple, more manageable components, often called 'modular' that can simplify the points of inter-actions. This takes us back to the principle of simplicity. Based on this principle, human individuals are highly sensitive to any discrepancy in their habits. The interest is aroused by any situation that appears

'too simple' to them. Leonardo da Vinci described it as *"the ultimate sophistication,"* while Albert Einstein said, *"everything should be made as simple as possible, but no simpler."*

Agile was born on the principle of simplicity, or 'kiss' principle—'keep it simple (stupid)'. Some organizations approach simplicity organically, building simple systems in parallel with the complex old ones. Others proceed to build simple systems on top of complex ones, making their systems even more complex. Products have just become victims of complex systems. Nothing could be changed or altered because the technology could not allow it. The life of the product would be deprived of growth and maintenance due to complex schedules of updating technologies that customers could not see.

As an example, consider remodeling your house and spending 90% of your time and money in replacing plumbing and electric wires, while the walls and floors will only get 10% of the investment. Customers see only 10%, exactly what is visible to them, the rest is buried investment.

The more value a product delivers to the customer, the better the chance to delight the customer. Agile introduced at least three simple concepts that resonated with product success: customer, value and speed. The simplicity with which agile as an execution method solves the problem of silos and centricity opens the door to cross-collaboration and openness. In the end, you can only make complex situations simple by decomposing them, breaking them down into smaller, more manageable parts that could be sized and measured.

Agile takes advantage of the decomposition method and decomposes big monolithic projects and structures to the level where everyone feels comfortable that they can be properly managed. And from there uncertainty is removed or properly dealt with, while visibility has increased and predictability, although unseemly, has evolved into consistency.

The Traditional Approach   **The Agile Approach**

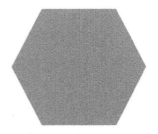 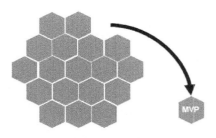

This product has so many features, I'm   It's so much better delivering this product
not sure I'll be able to deliver it!   in bite-sized pieces

Figure 2.6: Decomposition of Product Features

While agility got everyone to where they are today, it is not the end of the story. There is life beyond agile, although agile was only the necessary first step to see where product development and project management can work together and deliver on commitments. It may not be so foolish to believe that there is still room for improvement and that product owners can still alter processes and behaviors to achieve more with less. The new generation of product owners must keep their focus on value, so they can create and increase that value in everything they do. They will not only reduce waste but also build customer satisfaction and collect on their business strategies.

CHAPTER 3

CRASH THE CHALLENGES

*"It is not the most intellectual of the species that survives,
nor the most intelligent;
but the one most responsive to change."*
—Darwin

While Netflix was shipping out DVD's to their customer's homes, Blockbuster believed their physical stores were enough to please their customers. Blockbuster had been the leader of the movie rental market for years, and management did not see why they should change their strategy. Back in 2000, the founder of Netflix, Reed Hastings, proposed a partnership to the former CEO of Blockbuster, John Antioco. Netflix wanted Blockbuster to advertise their brand in the stores while Netflix would run Blockbuster's online store. The idea got turned down by Antioco because he thought it was ridiculous, and he felt that Netflix's business model was 'niche business'. Little did he know that Hasting's idea would have saved Blockbuster.

In 2010 Blockbuster filed for Chapter 11 bankruptcy protection, and Netflix is now a $28 billion-dollar company. The Forbes article that aptly describes what exactly happened to Blockbuster concluded that *"The Internet didn't kill Blockbuster, the company did it to itself"* (Denning, 2018).

Where is my Boss?

In Chapter 1, we introduced five challenges organizations must confront when delivering their strategy: culture, organization, focus, execution, and change. Inside organizations, product owners face the same challenges in their product delivery. In this chapter, we will discuss how leadership skills can help to address these challenges by empowering product owners to deal with organizational change, organizational culture, and benefits realization.

In Chapter 2, we introduced the concept of complexity and complicated organizations. To simplify the complexity of today's environment, organizations are using flexible structures. Leaders must empower product owners, allowing them to take ownership of their products.

The new generation of product owners needs to have basic leadership skills to develop their team and delegate to them, allowing them to take on additional responsibilities. Delegation—also referred to as empowerment—has many benefits:

- Simplify complex organizations by creating clear responsibilities;
- Create opportunities for team members to grow as employees making them more valuable;
- Free up time allowing the delegator to do higher-level work;
- Improve responsiveness to customers with faster and appropriate actions; and
- Make faster decisions since the person closest to the situation is making the decision.

Delegation is not easy to do as you are giving up control. The major concerns revolve around quality, time, and approach. The delegate (person being delegated to) may make mistakes or have resentment in doing the task. However, by not delegating, there will be no opportunity for staff to grow, and for leaders to focus on other priorities

and higher-level activities. The benefits of delegation, if done properly, will greatly outweigh any concerns.

Before delegating a task, product owners can use the Leadership Forces two-by-two matrix to identify the appropriate approach for delegation *(Leadership Forces, 2019)*. The Y-axis shows the level of support required, and the X-axis shows the level of direction required. The quadrant the person is in will determine which of the four delegation approaches to use:

- **Delegating**. Set up a formal transfer of responsibility with clear objectives and checkpoints.
- **Supporting**. Establish a clear way to respond to queries and clear roadblocks.
- **Coaching**. Support the person with frequent communication and encouragement.
- **Directing**. Provide specific tasks with frequent feedback.

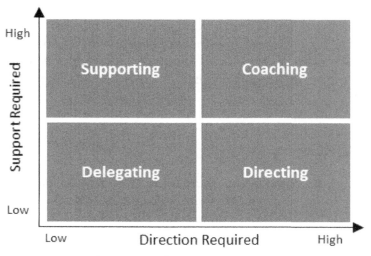

Figure 3.1: Delegation Approaches

As a product owner, you want to delegate as much as possible to your team. This way, you can build a team of professionals that will follow

the direction of customer care and product excellence. However, your organization needs to delegate product ownership and accountability to you first. For you to further ensure low direction and low support, you need to ensure you develop the skills to be a good product owner and get strategic direction for your products.

Delegation is situational based, you need to see if it is appropriate to delegate. Fitting the new tasks in people's busy schedules is always a concern when delegating. There are two approaches to delegating:

- **Commitment.** If you get a person's commitment to do the work, there is a much better chance the work will be done.
- **Technology.** Increasing the use of technology. You can delegate routine work to technology, for example, you can use a tool to report on task performance.

Lastly, as a product owner, you need to think about those cases when you delegate up to the supervisors or across to the peers. Although the delegating up or across follows the same process as to a direct report, it requires more care to position the reason for the delegation. You have to make sure that the person understands why they are better positioned to do the work than you. Before delegating a task to them, you should discuss the options and get their commitment.

When delegating a task, there are five steps that must be done *(Webb, 2017)*:

1. **Assess capabilities**. You want to make sure the delegate has the skills, capabilities, time, and interest to do the task. Delegating work to someone who does not have the necessary skills requires a coaching approach.

2. **Communicate**. You need to ensure the delegate understands the task, what must be done when it needs to be completed, what is the quality expectation and what is the budget.

66

3. **Support.** You want the delegate to know you are there to support them and guide them. Remember, you are delegating the task, not the responsibility.

4. **Establish checkpoints.** You need regular times to check in to review the process and discuss any issues that the delegate may be facing.

5. **Celebrate.** When the delegate finishes the task, you need to celebrate the success and reflect on lessons learned, a way to improve your delegation skills.

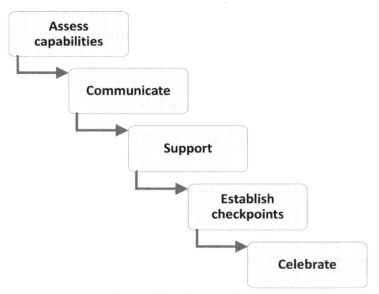

Figure 3.2: Delegation Steps

"As we assume more and greater responsibilities in our ascension through the ranks of leadership, naturally we can't keep doing the things we did two or even three positions ago" (Killelea, 2016). The right level of delegation is about finding the balance and depends on the level of maturity of your team, as well as the impact of the decisions made. Distributed control is only achieved when delegation is

pushed deeply into the organization, with constant communication and situational awareness.

As a product owner, to have true product ownership, you need to be the delegate for your product. For this to happen, three things have to be in place:

1. You need to have the time, which you can create by delegating tasks to your team;
2. You have to build the skills to own a product; and
3. Your organization needs to have the structure and the culture to support you.

Overcome the Unknown

Change is a fact of life. As a product owner, you are critical to your organization in delivering the strategy. To deliver strategy, an organization must deliver new products or new processes, forcing the organization to change. In some cases, the change is small; in other cases, it is a large endeavor called transformation. But ultimately, it is a change.

What happens to an organization that does not change? Think back to Chapter 1 and the Kodak example. For a variety of reasons. Kodak decided not to change when they had an opportunity to lead in the digital camera space. The result was they filed for Chapter 11 bankruptcy protection. Think about the taxi industry that did not listen to their customer's frustrations until Uber came along.

Regardless of its nature, change is an enabler for driving innovation and transformation. Depending on the number of change organizations can handle, there are three different types of changes organization could experience:

- **Change as an Evolution**. Solving complex problems, such as solving pollution, happens gradually through a process of satisfaction of the current state to trigger evolution to the next

state. For evolution change, there are triggering events based on time. When evolution reaches a trigger event, and there is customer acceptance, then the evolution proceeds towards the next trigger event. This process continues, and over time will go through stages of maturity and in some cases completion. Although at the start of the change process trigger events are established, these events can change over time to adapt to the changing environment. As a product owner, you can use this type of change when you want to evolve a product over time. For example, Apple and the development of the iPhone. When Apple first entered the portable music devices, they started with the iPod. Over time the iPod evolved to be connected to the Internet (iPod touch) to become smaller (iPod Nano), then to the iPhone and the iPad.

- **Change as a Transition**. The process of transition is another gradual change, bringing you through different phases from anxiety to happiness, fear to threats to joy, to depression, then from hostility to gradual acceptance, and then eventually moving forward and accepting the change. Transition is the approach preferred by organizations because it seems a gradual change with no major impacts. The focus is on taking small steps, get the organization on board with the changes, and continue from there. It is a great way to mitigate risks and manage expectations; however, change is slower, and going back to the original state is possible. As a product owner, you can use this type of change when you are introducing a new product and want to bring your customers along in small steps to gain their acceptance of the product. For example, your organization is implementing SAP, an enterprise reporting financial system that has several modules. To implement SAP in an organization you can introduce one or two modules to one or two departments at a time. Doing this, you allow the organization to get used to SAP in small pieces, so they are not overwhelmed.

- **Change as a Transformation**. The process of transformation is the most drastic one where there is no going back. Although many of the organizations do not know how to deal with transformations and because there is no feeling of safety, everybody is afraid and concerned about what the future will hold. Organizations going through transformations should encourage a 'fail fast learn fast' culture in which people can learn as much as possible and improve continuously. In transformations, the starting point is the trigger, and from there, the change is radical, as the past cannot be recognized and will never be mentioned. As a product owner, you would use this type of change when you must do a radical change to a product, and you cannot implement the change in increments—for example, Kodak. After the digital camera replaced the Kodak business model of film and paper, Kodak had no choice but to try to transform. Since Kodak filed for Chapter 11 bankruptcy protection in 2012, they had no choice but to adopt a transformation. Since 2012, Kodak, has tried several strategies and is still learning and trying the right mix of products to create sustained profitability.

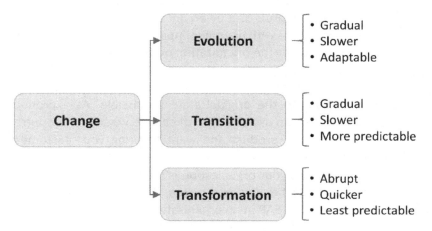

Figure 3.3: Types of Change

Fibernetics is a Canadian company that provides voice and data tele-communication solutions to residual and business customers. When John Stix was hired as President in early 2014, he realized the Fibernetics needed a change. The first task he assigned himself was to give his organization a thorough review—from the bottom to the top. After dedicating several weeks to the process, spending time with the individual departments, auditing meetings, having sit-downs in the cafeteria, or a beer with staff after work, his conclusions were two-fold: Firstly, the business, though successful, could be doing better. And secondly, it was the company's culture that was holding them back. The latter came as a surprise because, as one of the co-founders of the company, he had always felt that culture was one of Fibernetics' greatest strengths. That's why he took it upon himself in the second half of the year to introduce and deploy a new, more inclusive, empowering culture. To do this, Stix, used a change of transformation. Stix wanted the change to be done quickly, and since Fibernetics culture was changing drastically, it was not evolution or transition. Six months after the start of the change, Stix found that the effects of investing in company teammates, all 250 of them, had paid incredible dividends to the business and to the wellness on the company ecosystem. The impact on overall employee satisfaction and engagement has been tangibly represented by a marked increase in sales across all brands. Further, it has garnered strong press attention in the media, both locally and nationally in the Toronto Star that John has been asked to speak to other C-Level executives on what it means to be 'In' at Fibernetics. He sat down for an interview in his office to discuss culture, business, and decompressing under a boardroom table (*Taguiam, 2014*).

As a product owner, your product will trigger some type of change in your organization. You need to understand the change approach your organization is using so you can support it. You also need to think about your team and what changes are required for your team to be successful. We will discuss more how to implement change in Chapter 4. The new generation of product owners must focus on delivering value to their customers while communicating with them to ensure they are part of your product journey.

Overcome the Culture

One of the key barriers to implementing organizational change is overcoming the resistance of the organizational culture. A simple way to think of an organization's culture is 'how things are done around here'. An organization cannot afford to document every single process and procedure, thus the reliance on culture to get things done. A strong culture can improve the organization's efficiency as people know how to get the job done. However, if you are implementing change, the current culture will create resistance to the change and prevent it from being introduced. Remembering Peter Drucker's quote *"culture eats strategy for breakfast"*, if you want to implement strategy, you should figure out how to change the culture to support and deliver products.

The other interesting point about culture is that many organizations, especially larger ones, have multiple cultures. There can be different cultures depending on the location, the department, or the product. In some cases, the product owner may want to create a culture for the team to ensure the delivery of value to the customer. Value creating cultures build a network of customers and stakeholders who benefit from being around each other. You can only add new value when you protect what is already valuable to your customers. This means taking into consideration the contributions of all people in your network and building continuous improvement.

Tony Hsieh, the founder of Zappos, takes time every year to update his book *Delivering Happiness*, for his employees. The book tells the stories of how people feel about the company and how they take care of the culture, enforced over and over again (*Hsieh, 2013*). The Zappos model of hiring people based on cultural fit has been used as an example for many organizations. The value-driven culture at Zappos dictates whether people are a good fit for the organization or not. Even after selected, an employee must undergo a period of probation and training in a company's values and culture. At the end of this period, Zappos offers probationary employees an exit bonus in case

they are not ready to join Zappos, or the culture is not a good fit for them.

Figure 3.4: Types of Culture

The type of culture is defined based on two major components, the people vs. organization oriented on one axis and actuality vs. possibility achievement on the other axis. Based on these orientations, there are four major culture types:

- **Tribe or Clan.** Clan culture is a collaborative culture, more oriented towards a family environment. The leader in this culture is a clan or tribe chief, playing the role of a facilitator or mentor. The team is structured as a tribe, with teams that are working together, knowing everything that is happening in the other tribes. Transparency is a core value that drives the teams. In this culture, there is high morale, cohesion, commitment, communication, cultivation of people and development of products. Interactions and participation produce effectiveness. This type of culture is used in small family-run companies that are in very stable markets, such as law

firms, but larger organizations such as ING Netherlands have introduced a clan culture.

- **Adhocracy**. Adhocracy is a creative and entrepreneurial culture type. The leader is an innovator, entrepreneur, and visionary. This culture is characterized by flexibility, readiness, and agility, and the acquisition of people is based on cultural fit. Sometimes seen as a chaotic type of culture as people are self-organized. Zappos culture is focused on employee happiness, the stage where people become more creative, have more ideas, and identify themselves better with the environment they work in. *"Core values are the foundation of a sustainable and thriving culture. They act as a compass for how our team interacts with one another, with clients, and with our partners. Core values define who the organization is and how they make decisions." (Zappos Insights, 2019)*

- **Hierarchy**. Hierarchy is a controlling culture type of organization based on rules and regulations. The leader is a coordinator, director, and organizer. It enforces information management, reporting through communication, efficiency by plan, timelines, predictability, stability, and control. Control and efficiency make a capable process that can be predictable at all times. The type of culture is typical in large organizations and enforcement and emergency service agencies. In the police force, it is important that the police officers in the field follow the orders that they are given.

- **Market**. The market is a very competitive and achievement-oriented culture type. The leader is a hard driver, competitor, and producer. The focus is on planning, goal setting, and market share, while efficiency and profitability are priorities for this type of culture. Competing aggressively on the market with high customer focus is the key driver. Rivalry promotes productivity and improvement. Uber is an example of this type of culture where Uber aggressively moved into cities, in

some cases breaking regulations and city bylaws to compete with the taxi industry.

Product owners exist in all four types of culture. To be successful, the product owner needs to also adjust their leadership style to fit better within the organization's culture. This will allow the product owner to focus on measurable results and deliver value to the most important stakeholder, the customer.

The new generation of product owners needs to understand the culture of their organization and be able to shape the culture of their team to develop products that deliver value.

What is the Benefit?

As product owners, if you are to deliver value to your customers, then you need to understand what is meant by value. *"Value in business markets is the worth in monetary terms of the technical, economic, service, and social benefits a customer company receives in exchange for the price it pays for a marketing offering" (Narus, 2014).*

The definition highlights that delivering value means providing benefits to customers. As a product owner, you need to identify the benefits to be delivered by the product and ensure the benefits are realized. There are three steps to realizing benefits:

1. **Identify**. The first step in the benefits realization is to identify the benefits received by customers. The hard part is to identify how the benefit will be measured. Benefits are typically measured in monetary terms. With non-monetary benefits, such as brand recognition, staff retention, and corporate social responsibility this is especially hard. Another consideration with metrics is to ensure that any change in the metric is caused by the product benefit, but not other factors. For example, if, as a product manager you are enhancing a product and the metric is product revenue. After launch, revenue increases for your product. However, you notice that the

economy grew, and a competitor left the market. Was the revenue growth due to the product enhancement or the growth in the economy or the competitor exit? In this example, product revenue was not a good metric on its own.

2. **Deliver.** This step involves building and launching the product and collecting its benefits. As a product owner in this step, you need to monitor how the product is being received by the customer and, if any, upfront benefits that can be realized. You can use metrics in order to get a baseline and ensure you can collect the data before the product is introduced. Once you have collected data, then compare the results to the baseline and develop actionable steps to address the gaps.

3. **Sustain.** The final step is to ensure the benefits are realized over the long term. Continuous feedback from customers is being collected and measured, while sales are monitored for spikes and slowdowns. If the benefits are being realized, the product forecasts and objectives have been achieved. If not, the product owner needs to develop further actions, such as marketing campaigns, special offerings, deals, and special discounts, etc. to ensure the benefits are realized.

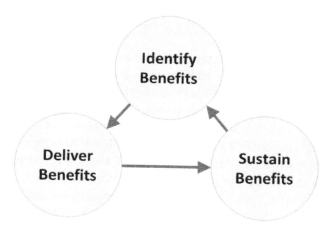

Figure 3.5: Benefits Realization

As a product owner, there are measurements that you can use to determine the value that customers receive. These measures include customer satisfaction surveys, customer satisfaction score (CSAT), net promoter score (NPS), customer effort score (CES), heat maps monitoring customers interactions with your digital products.

For customers, the benefit they get from a product is the difference between the value and the price they pay. This comparison can be made consciously or unconsciously, but in general, is done unconsciously.

Alice may be looking at purchasing a ticket to a sporting event. For a pre-season game, she could decide that the price of $20 for a ticket is too high. Watching a pre-season game when the team has no incentive to win has a low value for Alice. However, Alice may be willing to pay $500 for the same seat in the finals when the team has a chance to win the companionship. Same seat, but very different value for Alice.

As a product owner, you need to constantly communicate with customers to understand the benefits they receive from your product and what the value is. The new generation of product owners needs to take responsibility and accountability to own the products and to make the appropriate choices and decisions for their delivery. This means delegating tasks to the appropriate people, developing the skills to change, and forming a culture that will enable product management and ownership.

CHAPTER 4

HONE THE TEAM

"Coming together is a beginning; keeping together is progress; working together is success."
—Henry Ford

In traditional hierarchical organizations, managers direct the work of subordinates to ensure alignment with organizational strategic goals. Spans of control are limited to a reasonable number, typically ten people or fewer, so that managers can effectively oversee their subordinates' efforts. This organizational model can work well in business environments that are stable, where the pace of change is moderate and where annual planning cycles suffice for managing strategic changes and course corrections. In dynamic business environments, where innovation cycles happen in days or weeks, rather than months and years, and where much of the work is cross-functional in nature, this type of organizational model can be slow to respond and ineffective.

Organizations that take the approach of empowering autonomous teams must find ways to ensure that coordination and connectivity happen amongst those teams without relying on managers. Again, it is a matter of managerial art, as well as science, to achieve alignment without excessive control *(Garton, 2017)*.

SMART Teams

Over the past decade, five thousand executives from around the world were asked for feedback on what they think about their direct experiences in building powerful teams. The results are remarkably consistent and reveal three key dimensions of team building *(Keller, 2017)*:

- **Direction.** If there is a shared belief about what organizations are striving to achieve and the role of the team in getting there, the outcome is much favorable.

- **High-quality interactions.** If an interaction is characterized by trust, open communication, and a willingness to embrace conflict, it becomes high-quality and productive for the team.

- **Strong sense of renewal.** With a strong sense of renewal, team members are energized because they feel they can take risks and learn from outside ideas. They can achieve something that matters and often against the odds *(Keller, 2017)*.

The question is how to recreate the same conditions in every team and build a **SMART** team.

In 2013, Scotiabank, one of the top five Canadian banks, embarked on an amazing digital transformation adventure to reshape its financial service business. They were prepared to make dramatic strategic changes that no other Canadian bank had ever attempted. They visited banks from all over the world and learned from their successes and failures. Scotiabank's executive team committed to getting a separate digital project team called the Digital Factory, which would be located outside the core operations and build products based on the new agile way of working. It took Scotiabank many years and many iterations to build the originally envisioned team, but according to some team members and the market share results, the experiment was successful. Looking back at the achievements, some of the team members and leaders are still amazed at how a secluded, separate

organization like the Digital Factory has survived separately from Scotiabank for so many years. The future of Digital Factory is currently uncertain, but one thing is sure, it is targeted to be a SMART team, with a shared goal, motivated, accountable, respectful and trustworthy. For some of the Scotiabank teams who went through this transformation, the experience was unique. The team of approximately 300 people was able to work as an independent factory of launching products on-demand with customer focus in mind. Newly created and specialized product owners joined the agile teams and worked side by side with the development team to build the new products. Of course, the Digital Factory model is not even near to perfection, but the concept was itself groundbreaking for a major bank and laid the foundation for core transformations. The journey continues and is an example of how organizations empower their people and build teams that would work for common goals.

General Stanley McChrystal explains in his book *Team of Teams* how he was able to build trust and maintain an environment of mutual respect. In his special task force, McChrystal made individuals realize the importance of being connected with the rest of the task force to defeat the enemy. A group of individuals does not become a team until they form an entity where there are common goals, shared values, trust, reliability on one another and happiness. In his book, McChrystal introduces the concept of a 'team of teams' as an organization within which the relationships between constituent teams resemble those between individuals on a single team. Teams that have traditionally resided in separate silos would now have to become fused by trust and purpose. Coordinating multiple teams and having them working together for a common purpose is one of the major leadership challenges for organizations planning to scale their new ways of working. Building an agile team that works separately in the organization to deliver 'right in time' products to customers is one thing; having multiple such teams depending on each other and supporting each other for the same purpose is much more challenging. McChrystal formed a big communication room where he allowed everyone to participate. Everyone who was interested in attending the update meeting, which was secret before, could. Like the Digital

Factory, McChrystal's Task Force, an expensive central space similar to Bloomberg's bullpen, was an environment of transparency and trust where people could contribute their knowledge to the same purpose, defeating the enemy, in this case, Al-Qaeda. The teamwork allowed people to link their missions and ideas, build big-picture plans, and work together instead of working in silos *(McChrystal, 2015)*.

For a product owner to successfully deliver value to their customers, they need to create a **SMART** team. A **SMART** team has five characteristics:

- **S**hared goals. A team with a purpose that is shared and agreed amongst its members is going in the same direction. Asking 'Why are we here?' is probably the best way to start building these goals. The product owner, as a leader, can work with the team to create that shared purpose and build the internal drive in the team to accomplish its mission, even if it seems to be impossible. People do not want to come to work and do something that any other team could accomplish. They want to do something extraordinary and be recognized that they can do the work. Doing something competent helps people build confidence and satisfaction with work resulting in higher engagement and pride.

  Establishing clear goals allows for the identification of the measures of success that build a purpose and a plan for what work matters most. The measurements should show progress and serve to focus on team efforts. If this is done correctly, distractions are kept to a minimum, and everyone can be allowed to contribute at their best. Once the goals are shared and agreed with the team, product owners need to share the goals with the rest of the departments, therefore aligning them to the strategic goals of the organization.

- **M**inimum supervision. Agile introduced the concept of self-managed teams as a way of expressing the team's accountability to perform tasks independently. Agile teams emphasize

the team composition and the team needs to be kept small. Research suggests that the team's effectiveness starts to diminish if there are more than ten people on it *(Keller, 2017)*. This makes perfect sense if you consider the communication formula for calculating the number of communication channels $[n(n-1)/2]$ in a team. Larger teams have incrementally more communication channels, which negatively impacts decision-making and productivity. These teams also undermine ownership of good decisions as there is no time for everyone to be heard. Thinking beyond the team size, organizations should consider what complementary skills and attitudes each team member brings to the table, whether they recognize improvement opportunities or feel accountable for the entire company's success, not just their business area. The attitude is everything in small or large teams to work together towards shared values.

Large organizations often cannot limit their teams to just ten or fewer members due to too much complexity to manage work. The CEO of a global insurance company had 18 direct reports spread around the globe. The video conference meetings could rarely discuss any single subject for more than 30 minutes because of the size of the agenda. The CEO, therefore, formed three top teams: one to deal with organization strategy and the long-term health of the company; another one that handled shorter-term performance and operational issues; and the third assigned with governance policy and people-related issues. Some executives, including the CEO, sat on each other's meetings, not only on one. With that, some members could choose to bring indirect reports from the next level of management down as the CEO recognized the importance of having the right expertise in the room, introducing new people with new ideas, and coaching the next generation of leaders.

- **A**ccountable. Self-managing leads to increased accountability as team members feel more empowered in making decisions and own them. The product owner is an accountable role to prioritize the backlog for the product features and to make sure that the team is working on the highest priority items. Moreover, the product owner meets with the customer to collect feedback and generate more features to add to the product.

  An accountable team will avoid repeatable mistakes and ensure that everyone works together to achieve success. Any failures are taken seriously by the team as learning for future improvements. Startups allow their employees to fail as soon as possible so they can use the failures as sources for knowledge. The proof of concepts or experiments are prerequisites for starting product enhancements, where team members prove the viability of the product or service before proceeding to develop the final version.

- **R**espectful. A **SMART** team is a team that respects each other's time and space and appreciates when everyone on the team is working towards the same goal. With respect comes accountability, and with accountability comes successful delivery. Respect is hard to build and very easy to lose; therefore, the team must continually work on building respect. The product owner always needs to maintain a positive and cool attitude, especially in situations of crisis and conflict. The key to building respect is to build relationships with the team members and be close to the team. The proximity of the team introduced by the agile principle states people's interactions are preferred over documentation, helps teams interact more, therefore building respect and empathy.

  In building respect, there are three levels. The first level is **tolerance** by accepting each other the way they are. Coming from diverse backgrounds and different departments, a team

is formed on the premise of diversity to improve innovation and creativity. The second level is **civility**, where team members behave civilly with each other, especially in situations of conflict. The third level is **high regard** when team members appreciate knowledge, expertise and pure advice from each other. Product owners should and must strive to create high in for team members, gain credibility within the team and bring the best advice to them.

- **T**rustworthy. It is not a coincidence that trust is the last characteristic of a **SMART** team. Trust within the team and with other stakeholders is probably the most important value of a team. A team needs to communicate quickly and respond rapidly to changes as they build the products. Not having enough trust amongst team members can waste effort and energy for people to look for blame and cover their tracks. A climate of trust provides the foundation for effective team interactions, being able to sprint to delivering value. By paying attention to team interactions, credibility, respect, and behaviors, product owners can encourage and accelerate trustworthiness among team members and stakeholders.

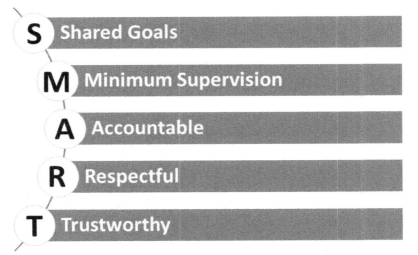

Figure 4.1: SMART Teams

In his book named *The Five Dysfunctions of a Team*, Patrick Lencioni creates a model in which trust is the foundation for all other constructive behaviors such as results-focused, accountability, commitment, and conflict *(Lencioni, 2012)*. Without trust, there is no common accountability, goals, commitment and creative conflict management.

A **SMART** team has all the ingredients and meets all criteria for being an Agile team focused on product delivery. The secret component is obtaining the buy-in from the organization's executive team and having them be part of the team. Executives whose organizations have been through agile transformations say much the same thing. In an interview with McKinsey, Scott Richardson, chief data officer at Fannie Mae, said, *"Creating a new team is probably the most important thing managers can do, so make sure you get it right. When we created our initial agile teams, I was personally involved with structuring them and selecting team members. It might sound crazy to get so involved in this level of detail, but it is critical that the early teams become true beacons for success"* (Kaur, 2017). Choosing high-caliber people not only sets up the teams to be successful but also teaches managers how to build more independent teams. *"By the fourth or fifth team,"* Richardson continued, *"my direct reports knew what questions to ask and how to structure a proper team, and they could scale up on their own from that point forward"* (Kaur, 2017).

The Leader in You

Spotify was not the first online entrant to online music services, but it was an innovator in marketing approaches, technology, and subscription options that have enabled it to become a market leader in music subscription. The first major entrant in the online music services was Napster in 1999. Napster in its initial formation was the first widely used service for 'free' peer-to-peer (P2P) music sharing service. The record companies mounted a legal challenge against Napster due to lost revenues on music sales, and Napster was eventually forced to close its business. The Napster brand was purchased following bankruptcy in 2008 and created its second organization offering

legal music. Now Napster focuses on the music subscription service as part of the Rhapsody music services in direct competition to Spotify.

Spotify learned very early how to be a leader in the online music market. Their famous alternative management model, based on servant leadership and interaction-based learning, allowed them to grow fast and attract the right talent. Spotify structured their teams into 'squads,' which are 'loosely coupled, but tightly aligned' teams, and has become a model for several organizations, including ING Netherlands. A squad is a self-organized and cross-functional team of no more than eight people with all the tools they require to perform their work effectively. Each squad is accountable for a discrete aspect of the product and works to release it in the hands of the customer. A collection of squads is called a tribe, a community of about 50-150 people sharing a 'habitat' overseen by a tribe lead and a tribe leadership team. Tribes are comprised of several squads linked together through chapters, which is a horizontal grouping that helps to support specific competencies such as quality assistance, agile coaching, and web development. The chapter's primary role is to facilitate learning and competency development throughout the squads *(Garton, 2017)*.

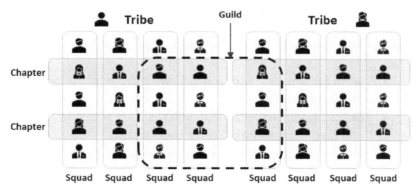

Figure 4.2: The Tribe at Spotify

"The reporting structure is upside down here at Spotify: team members are supported by leaders, not the other way around. Leaders do

not tell team members what to do, and team members tell leaders what they need! Leaders help team members to figure out what the organization needs to do next. This is the core mindset that reflects itself in our model, commonly known as servant leadership," says Kristian Lindwall, Team Lead and Agile Coach at Spotify *(Lindwall, 2018).*

Spotify believes in the player-coach model where Chapter leaders are also squad members. Squad members can switch squads and retain the same formal leader within their Chapter. Spotify introduced a third organizational element, known as a Guild. Guilds are lightweight communities of interest whose primary purpose is to share knowledge in areas that cut across Chapters and Squads, such as leadership, continuous delivery, and web delivery.

Cross-functional teams are more likely to emerge leaders due to extended accountability and autonomy in the work they perform. As Noel Tichy said, *"Leadership is about change ... the best way to get people to venture into the unknown terrain is to make it desirable by taking them there in their imagination." (Weil, 2012).*

Leadership is about making and embracing change in any possible way with people at every level of the organization, trying new ways of working, and enforcing positive attitudes. There are many studies on leadership styles. For this book, five leadership styles will be used. Each leadership style identifies the level of flexibility individuals have versus their delivery focus. The five leadership styles are:

- **Servant.** Leaders 'with a heart' who listen to the people in the team and their ideas.
- **Laissez-faire.** Leaders allow their teams to focus on activities and take full responsibility for their actions.
- **Charismatic.** Leaders energize the team and other stakeholders with enthusiasm.
- **Transactional.** Leaders have a hands-on delivery focus to achieve results.

- **Transformational.** Leaders use their communication, credibility, and visionary abilities to drive towards an inspiring future.

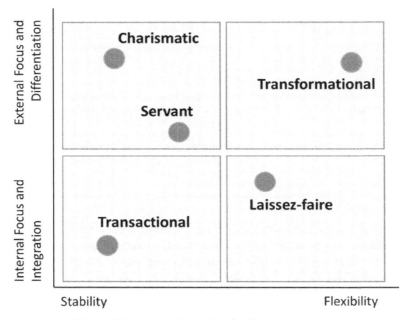

Figure 4.3: Leadership Styles for Product Owners

Product owners, like all leaders, can apply any of the five leadership styles in the most appropriate situation. Here are some examples of typical product owner leadership situations and the leadership style that would be the most appropriate. Of course, every situation is different, and product owners need to know how to switch leadership styles as required.

Situation	Leadership style
Reviewing the product backlog with the team and assigning tasks to the user stories	**Transactional**: Product Owners ensure all tasks are assigned and the team members know what must be done.
Receiving customer feedback and building the backlog	**Transformational**: Product owners can understand the feedback and transform it into backlog items.
Dealing with situations of conflict between two team members	**Servant**: Product Owners create an environment of trust and support the team members in resolving the conflict.
Team members are working on the tasks	**Laissez-faire**: Product Owners let the team do their work as defined and clear roadblocks as required.
Selling ideas to the customers	**Charismatic**: Product Owners convince customers that the solution provided will address the customers' concern

Table 4.1: Situational Leadership for Product Owners

Product owners should provide an inspiring vision with a validated product strategy that communicates the product value proposition. The product owner is the person who champions the product, who facilitates the product decisions, and who has the final say about the product.

Change is Everywhere

Everything around us changes every day, and the speed of change is higher by the day. Agile is based on the assumption that circumstances change as the product develops. That's why, in an agile iteration, the planning, design, development, and testing are done in small cycles and continue as the product takes form. The agile team continuously manages changes by making sure they are working through the product life cycle. The features may change or be replaced by the product owner or by the customer, to ensure the goal of customer satisfaction. Change is no longer controlled but managed to ensure business objectives are being met, and the product delivers value to the customer.

Resistance to change can arise from the fear of the unknown, not understanding why the change is needed, a lack of trust in those wanting to change, poor communication, or change in the routine. To survive, an organization must change to face the competition, adopt new technologies, and deliver value to customers. Product owners need to understand how to implement change in their organization.

Jason Little has adopted the Kubler-Ross model of grief in terminal illness to reflect seven stages that people go through when navigating organizational change *(Little, 2014)*. The stages go through a rise, fall, and rise again of morale and competence. The seven stages are:

1. **Shock.** Surprise or shock at the event and that a change is even being suggested.

2. **Denial.** Disbelief, looking for evidence that the need for change is not true. People always talk about the change until it affects them personally.

3. **Frustration.** Recognition that things are going to be different, sometimes people are angry. Why is this change happening to me? Why do I need to change?

4. **Depression.** Low mood and lack of energy. There is a lack of understanding, and people feel overwhelmed, possibly leading to depression.

5. **Experiment.** Initial engagement with the new product or process. With the new engagement, morale starts to improve.

6. **Decision.** Learn how to work with the new product or process and feeling more positive. Morale improves as confidence grows.

7. **Integration.** Change is fully integrated, and people accepting the change. If done well, morale and competence are higher than at the start of the process.

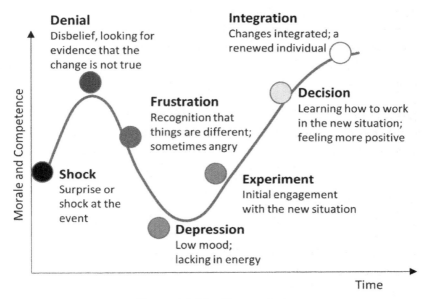

Figure 4.4: The Change Cycle

Jeff Hiatt developed the **ADKAR** model to guide individuals and organizations through change *(Hiatt, 2003)*. The model has five steps:

1. **A**wareness of the need for change. Product owners, you must ensure that everyone involved with the product understands why the change is required, what the change is going to address, and how it will add more value.

2. **D**esire to support the change. Product owners must ensure that the people involved with the product or impacted by the change are fully supportive.

3. **K**nowledge of how to change. Product owners must ensure the team members have the knowledge and skills to do the new tasks.

4. **A**bility to demonstrate skills and behaviors. Product owners must ensure team members have the knowledge they need to practice and demonstrate work proficiency.

5. **R**einforcement to ensure the change sticks. Product owners must ensure people only adopt a new process or use a new product that is linked to the benefits of the change.

On June 1, 2009, General Motors (GM) was in a crisis and filed for Chapter 11 bankruptcy protection. GM problems started long before 2008. In the 1980s, GM started to lose market share to the Japanese automotive manufacturers. Initially, there was shock by GM that North American customers would abandon the North American designed and manufactured cars. However, GM continued to make money and moved into the denial stage. Then in 2008, the financial crisis hit, and car sales dropped; GM had no response. They were just frustrated by a financial crisis that had impacted them. GM realized they had to change the company to survive. Specifically, GM needed to:

- *Reduce the number of dealers in North America to align with sales;*
- *Reduce labor cost by negotiating union contracts;*
- *Reduce the number of models to reduce costs and brand conflict;*
- *Introduce new models to align with the market demands; and*
- *Obtain financing from the government to fund the transition.*

During this period, GM moved from frustration in not being able to make the change to depression with what had to be done. The last step was the filing for bankruptcy protection, which allowed GM to reorganize and to start implementing their plans. From 2010 to 2014, GM moved through the experimentation and decision stages into integration, and in 2013, GM's stock was back on the S&P500 index after being removed in 2009.

Product owners have a key role in continuously improving their products to deliver value to customers. To do this, product owners must

change their product, the way the product is delivered and supported. Product owners are implementing change! To be effective the new generation of product owners needs to be able to understand the change cycle and how to help move their team through the stages of change with minimal disruption. The new generation of product owners must be prepared to disrupt the status quo of their product, focus on the growth stage of the product life cycle, and allow changes to disrupt your process of enhancing products.

As a product owner, your primary focus is completing the product and delivering value. But, the greatest challenge for the product owner is user adoption of the product. As a leader, you need to be able to lead your team and customers through change. One of the techniques is to use the 'ready, willing and able' phrase *(Inniss, 2019):*

- **Willing**. 'I want to do this.'
- **Able**. 'I know how to do this.'
- **Ready**. 'Okay, let's do this'/ 'I am going to do this.'

No matter how hard you want the change to happen, think about the customer and the amount of change they need to absorb, balanced with the amount of time it will take for them to understand the change. Many products fail for not considering the right elements of change management when development in launching products.

When Sears finally transformed their stores in Canada to respond to the growth of online vendors, it was too late and done too fast at the same time. The new model worked in other stores like Winners or Marshalls but did not work for Sears. The amount of change was too much to absorb for the frequent Sears customers used to a certain 'Sears' experience. Nor was the change friendly to the customer service employee who was absorbing a lot of organizational processes and leadership changes. In the end, the new model pushed Sears to its grave forever.

Sears tried to do a transformational change; successful organizations are transforming over time while gradually introducing change and bringing their customers along with them in their journey.

Culture Breaks; Culture Builds

The topic of culture has been exhausted in the last years or so because the culture is one of the most important things that need to happen from a changed perspective in organizations. Quotes such as *"culture eats strategy for breakfast"* (Peter Drucker) or *"Corporate culture matters"* (Simon Sinek) have been making the headlines for years. Organizations need to think about people and have people in the center of their operations to introduce rapid learning and fast decision-making. The culture game, however, is still a game being played by all organizations trying to implement many changes without changing anything in their way of working. The result is in the failure stories that will be told by the generations to come.

Culture is about having organizations make rapid changes and be able to adapt quickly to any external impacts while having employees prone to accept new situations that may cause disruptions. Internal training and continuous enforcements are necessary to coach employees on how to deal with situations of uncertainty. Change is not so much about processes and tools as it is about the culture of the people and how they behave in situations of constant change.

The culture of the new generation of product owners, as leaders of the team, is a culture of inclusion and productivity. The product culture complements the organization's culture in the sense that it contributes to the delivery of a successful outcome. The product culture is no longer temporary, and it extends beyond project culture having a life of its own, focused on growing a sellable product.

There are five principles of product culture:

- **Customer-driven mission**. Focus on getting the customer to buy the offered products

- **Outcome over output or processes.** Focus on the actual outcome, including the benefits or value that the products deliver.
- **Leadership over management.** Focus on leading the team and setting the vision instead of managing activities for the teams.
- **Team over function or task.** Focus on the people, less on the task or function being performed.
- **Technology as a core asset.** Focus on getting the technology to enable the work, but growing the products and services being offered.

Google has used the five principles of product culture to build its success, starting with its customer-driven mission, "organize the world's information and make it universally accessible and useful." Google is focused on outcomes. Google has also displayed a very low barrier to launching new products and might be a technology company that has launched and killed the highest number of products. In part, this is due to the use of data Google collects on products used. Google is famous for its management framework using 'Objectives and Key Results' (OKRs). Management through OKRs involves setting priorities in the form of 'objectives' (for example, 'Improve new user onboarding'), and defining measurable 'key results' that determine whether progress toward the objective was made (for example, 'increase completion rate of the signup flow from 80% to 85%'). The culture at Google is a team culture, where people work on flexible schedules, are encouraged to be creative and build a fun environment for themselves and the team. The use of technology to collect and analyze data using tools such as Google Analytics for websites drives Google's product development and business model. (Goetzman, 2019).

On top of that, the product culture is a culture of delivering value which has the following four principles:

- **Efficiency.** The team takes every opportunity to reduce waste

- **Collaboration**. Team members work together for the success of the product, and there is team spirit
- **Value**. The focus is on delivering the features with the highest value to customers, and everything else is noise
- **Flow**. Keeping the customer happy while continuously delivering features that are needed

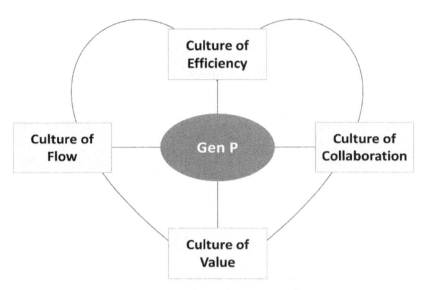

Figure 4.5: Value Delivery Principles

The new generation of product owners must create a team culture that fits in the organization's culture while supporting the five principles of product culture (customer-driven mission, outcome over output or processes, leadership over management, team over function or task, and technology is a core enabler) and four principles of value delivery culture (efficiency, collaboration, value, and flow). This can be achieved by being effective leaders, using the appropriate leadership styles to ensure alignment of the team members to the product culture. A team culture that will deliver value to customers!

To transition the team to a culture focused on products and value delivery, Norm Sabapathy has developed a ten-step process to change the culture of an organization *(Folz, 2016):*

1. Define a set of values and behaviors that you want to have in place.

2. Align the culture with the strategy, processes, structure, and leadership.

3. Connect culture to accountability to ensure that team members are going to be accountable for their behaviors.

4. Have visible proponents of the culture for people's behaviors.

5. Define the non-negotiables by identifying unacceptable behaviors and have consequences that are applied.

6. Align your culture with your brand to ensure a consistent message within and outside your organization.

7. Measure it, there is the saying 'you get what you measure.' When you measure the change in the culture you can see the progress and be able to celebrate successes, which helps to accelerate the change.

8. Do not rush it as it takes time to change the culture.

9. Invest time and leadership to change the culture. The sooner you start, the sooner the culture will be changed, and you can deliver greater value.

10. Be bold and lead, as a leader, make the bold step and show leadership to ensure your product is going to be successful.

Netflix created a competitive culture that is authentically true to it-self, one that attracts the type of talent it needs for the type of am-bition it has. Netflix attributes its success in part to this unique cul-ture. *"Many current and former employees credit it with keeping the company stocked with high performers capable of fast decision-mak-ing. This, they say, allows for a nimbleness that has helped it disrupt the global TV and movie industries" (Denning, 2018).* The most inno-vative cultures are rarely comfortable. Comfort is found in compla-cency. Pushing boundaries breeds discomfort. It may surprise detrac-tors that some people willingly choose to sign up for such a bumpy ride.

The new generation of product owners is a leader. You need to de-velop a **SMART** team, leading the team through change and ensure the product has an appropriate culture to deliver value to customers. This includes choosing any framework that makes you and your prod-uct successful.

ITERATE TO MAKE IT HAPPEN

"What good is an idea if it remains an idea?
Try. Experiment. Iterate. Fail. Try again.
Change the world."
—Simon Sinek

It is not innovation that sets Silicon Valley apart from other centers of technological development—it is a willingness to iterate, get feedback, learn, and adapt. After all, even Hewlett and Packard, the spiritual godfathers of Silicon Valley, got their start building audio oscillators for Disney, a technology that had first been developed more than 40 years before. More recently, well-established tech companies have spun out start-ups such as Quora, leveraging both human capital and product development experience to improve execution on pre-existing concepts. In Quora's case, the founders were not the first to build an Internet answers site but instead were able to draw from their experience working at Facebook to apply a Facebook-style user interface to the well-known questions and answers (Q&A) format *(Upbin, 2014).*

Iterate. Increment. Transform.

Iteration is the process of transforming your product based upon the way customers respond to your business. Because this requires a

great deal of attentiveness, it is usually viewed as a process that is perfect for small, tech-savvy startup companies. However, there are examples of iterations involving a slow, steady change in a predictable direction over many years. The National Geographic Society published its first magazine in 1888. In 1914, they introduced color photographs of animals and locations from all over the world. By the end of the 20th century, National Geographic recognized that the market was changing and started to introduce new products such as the National Geographic channel. On its TV channel, National Geographic also changed its reality series mix to meet the interests of new generations of viewers. Through iterations, National Geographic transformed itself from a publisher of a yellow-bound magazine to showcase their award-winning photographs on television, social media, and photo-sharing sites *(Roos, 2014)*.

Other examples of iteration can be quite revolutionary and transformational. YouTube started as a dating site until it changed its mission and purpose entirely. Regardless of where your organization falls on the spectrum, it is likely there was some form of iteration used in your organization's history. However, most organizations lose the willingness to adapt and incrementally grow as soon as they find success. This is probably the biggest mistake they make. About three months before the public launch of the iPhone, Apple CEO Steve Jobs sent the design team back to the drawing board because of flaws in the product's design. James Dyson created more than 5,000 failed prototypes of his wildly successful Dyson vacuum cleaner. For organizations to be successful, to address the challenges of technology and business models, they must continuously change through iterations and ultimately transform their operations *(Anthony, 2014)*.

In recent years, iterative development methods have proven to be the most suitable for software product development, especially mobile and web applications. In software product development, technologies and trends are changing and advancing rapidly. The iterative process provides the ability to quickly adapt to the changing environment, not related as much to technology, but rather to user feedback. For some businesses, having small changes implemented in

their product is the most effective way to produce a huge impact. The iterations keep customers engaged if the feedback is considered while preserving brand identity. If the small tweaks fail, the impact should not be too great, with the right precautions. However, if they succeed and compound, the rewards can be monumental. During the recession of 2008, Procter & Gamble (P&G) slightly changed its business model to reach a wider customer base with a broad price range of products. They developed both super-premium products that were sold at a higher price premium than current products and value products that appealed to cost-conscious customers. With these small changes, P&G delivered higher profits, although sales stayed relatively low.

Iterations are short duration phases, often one to four weeks, where teams select a couple of their customers, the most important stories, and complete them as working products. When products are incrementally done, the customer gets an enhanced product they can test and appreciate. This is also a great way to track the progress of adding value by measuring the rate at which the team can turn stories into production-ready products. Imagine you have a backlog with ten features for your customers. From this backlog, you, the new generation of product owners, can plan how many iterations you can implement to clear the backlog. In the first iteration, you with your team select features 1, 4, and 5. In the second iteration, you select features 2 and 6 as they are larger ones and in the third iteration, you select the remaining features. This way you will be incrementally delivering features to your customers. Also, if you find that customer feedback tells you that customers value feature 3 more than feature 2, you can adjust the order and replace feature 2 with feature 3 in the second iteration. The scope of the iterations is variable, and it changes based on customer feedback. Every iteration will allow you to assess how the team has been doing developing the features, the customer feedback, and the product that you want to release to the customer. Each iteration is built upon the last iteration and the lessons learned from all previous iterations. As iterations are completed to develop the product, the effort decreases, and fewer features are remaining on the backlog.

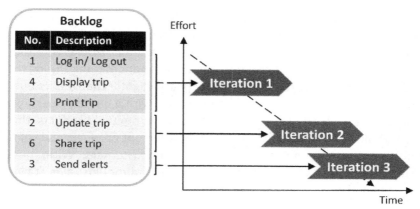

Figure 5.1: The Agile Plan

Multiple iterations are required to build all the features of the product. Iteration approaches can vary between different methods. Scrum is a popular framework that is defined by iterations called sprints. In Scrum, sprints are typically two weeks long and can vary between one to four weeks in length. A sprint is bookmarked by formal meetings, with product development work being taken on at the beginning, while completed and ready for review at the end. The sprint is advanced by daily meetings where the progress of the work is discussed. Products are built in releasable increments as requested by the product owners or customers.

Extreme programming (XP) is like Scrum, as iterations typically last around two weeks. The XP approach provides the time frame for product development work to be completed, but the primary focus is on how the work is completed. XP gives a restrictive framework for how to develop and implement the product development work, adapting the changes requested by the customer.

Kanban is another common method, and it is defined by continuous flow. Features are prioritized in a backlog with tasks that are taken on by the team as they have the capacity. The work remains in progress until it is completed and accepted by the product owner. Kan-

ban tasks may not have specific starting and stopping points; however, it will be helpful to see when a task started and monitor the time it took to complete. This will give the product owner a way of estimating the work with the team in the future. Although it does not have pre-defined iterations, Kanban is considered iterative through cadences, as the work can be constantly changed and improved based on continuous feedback. While Scrum and XP are designed for the software industry, Kanban can be used for all industries. Toyota adopted Kanban in the 1940s as an inventory management system.

The Fortune 500 issue published a story about Amazon.com. *"It's easy to believe that Jeff Bezos is one of the great innovators,"* the story noted. *"But that's not exactly the case. His rise into Fortune 500-dom has little to do with innovation and more to do with iteration."* The only way to successfully innovate is to be prepared to iterate over-and-over again. Amazon is a successful innovator because of its focused iteration approach. That focus has allowed it to hone its core disruptive e-tailing business model and expand into new markets like supporting third-party retailing and Amazon Web Services *(Anthony, 2014)*.

It is hard to invent something completely new in today's world, and yet the real mark on innovation is made by those willing to experiment and fail fast, iterate experimentally and execute effectively. The key is to identify and solve new problems with new versions of successful inventions.

Airbnb was not the first online short-term housing rental service. Among others, VRBO launched in 1996 (which HomeAway acquired in 2006), Couchsurfing.org launched in 1999, and Craigslist had a long history of matching apartment renters with sub lessors. However, Airbnb was successful, not because of the tweaked idea (a network of bed and breakfasts), but rather because of a series of small iterations, from a well-designed interface to a low-barrier of entry that opened up a new 'passive' marketplace. By incorporating user reviews, profiles, and an in-house private messaging system, buyers and sellers can match property owners and customers more efficiently, without

having to do extensive background work and due diligence. Airbnb's success is, therefore, intimately tied to social networking, drawing heavily upon the dual influences of Facebook-style personal profiles and degrees of separation to eBay-style approval ratings. In this sense, Airbnb was not only iterative in its business model, but also in its implementation (Upbin, 2014).

James Hong, a co-founder of Hot or Not and an angel investor, said *(Upbin, 2014): "For many start-ups, the confluence of iterative product development and sound execution leads to success—not just the initial idea."* Anyone can have ideas; few are being developed and iterated to achieve full maturity and become products. As the new generation of product owners, whether you are working in a startup, building your startup, or working for a large organization, you must use iterative approaches to create an impact on acquisition, retention, and monetization of your customers. The new generation of product owners take actions and demonstrate changes are possible, while feedback from failures is lessons for success. Iterative approaches prove that time favors the team. A product development team can now start working on the product as soon as some items in the backlog are defined to create the minimum value to customers, and then based on feedback define the next set of features to enhance the product.

The new generation of product owners must continuously add new features to their products through iterations based on customer feedback. Through incremental changes, their products will be transformed, continuing to deliver sustainable value.

It Starts with the Backlog …

Every iteration starts with defining the scope, capabilities, and features that need to be completed to create a product. A product backlog is a product scope with a purpose. The features in a backlog can be split and prioritized in many ways while remaining flexible for the team to be able to come back as many times as they want to the

backlog of select features. Contrary to the scope in predictive or waterfall methodology where the features are defined at the start of the product development, in an iterative or adaptive approach, the scope is refined and changed frequently. Features are being removed or added to the backlog as the product owner sees fit based on the customer feedback and interactions. The team can also propose features for removal and deletion to the product owner based on the experience they are having with the product development. Customers and other stakeholders can also participate in backlog refinement based on their feedback. A backlog is a living bucket of features that can be implemented in any future iteration. The main purpose of the backlog is to prioritize feedback from multiple sources, especially from the customer, to enhance the product and add value for customers.

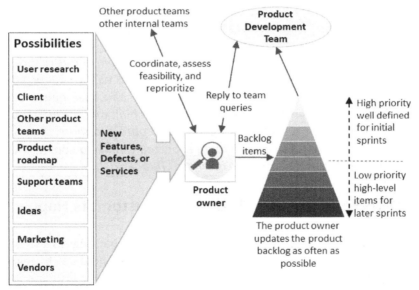

Figure 5.2: Backlog Prioritization

The product owner is the funnel that takes all the requests and creates features that are, analyzed, prioritized, and placed in the backlog. Once that is done, the product owner and the team discuss the features and re-prioritize them based on input from the team on delivery commitments and estimates of capacity. The team can plan

these backlog items into iterations and can get to work right away. Only high priority high-value items are estimated and planned; the low priority low-value ones will wait in the queue until the team has the bandwidth to execute them. Some of the low priority items will never get to the execution line, being dropped from the list. This way, the team can focus on the most valuable items and avoid any distractions.

The number one piece of advice that startup founders received from those who mentor venture capitalists and even their peers is to iterate, iterate, iterate. Yet it seems difficult for organizations to find their iterative rhythm and keep it.

When Jorge Heraud and Lee Redden started Blue River Technology, they were students at Stanford. They had a vision of building robotic lawn mowers for commercial spaces. After talking to over 100 customers in 10 weeks, they learned their initial customer target—golf courses—did not value their solution. Then they began to talk to farmers and found a huge demand for an automated way to kill weeds without chemicals. Filling the farmers' needs became their new product focus, and within 10 weeks, Blue River had built and tested a prototype. Nine months later, the start-up had obtained more than $3 million in venture funding. The team expected to have a commercial product ready just nine months after that (Blank, 2013).

Own Your Stories … They Make Customers Happy

Story mapping is an effective tool to build product backlogs in a structural, visual way, engaging the participating stakeholders. It helps build a shared understanding, identify and discuss gaps, visualize interdependencies, and perform better sizing. Story mapping may also help planning the release activities by understanding the amount of change that will be introduced to the organization.

Story mapping is a top-down approach of defining 'personas', activities and tasks and is represented as a tree. Story mapping starts with

an overarching vision for the product that will achieve customer objectives or goals. These objectives are reached by identifying features and epics that can be further decomposed into stories. To complete the stories for product development, the user needs to perform tasks that can be assigned to a group of stories belonging to the same epic to ensure dependencies between tasks are properly identified and managed. User tasks are the basic elements of a story map because they ultimately complete the stories.

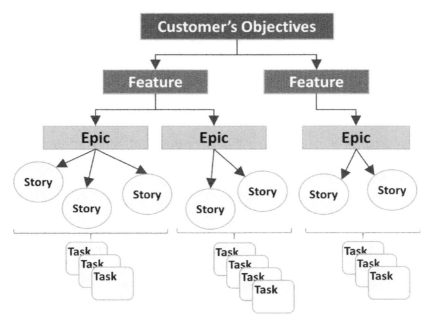

Figure 5.3: Story Map (Goal, Activity, Task, Stories)

An online store has a goal for customers to be able to find a product quickly. To achieve the goal of 'Find a product,' there are multiple features such as 'Browse through product category,' 'Free text search,' 'Promoted products.' Looking at the first approach 'Browse through product category,' to build the story map, epics can be defined as 'Search' and then subsequent stories and tasks associated with that epic. A user needs to perform certain tasks such as enter

product category, click the search icon, etc. Story maps help decomposing big stories as customers and product owners tell them while finding holes in the story flow.

There are many advantages of story mapping:

- Provides a view of the iteration size to build commitment on the work
- Fosters collaboration and builds shared understanding
- Helps prioritization of the scope, into 'very important,' 'important' and 'nice to have' based on the importance of the value they generate
- Visualizes all the work on a physical or electronic board to help the team size the stories quickly, and
- Helps stakeholders understand the complexity of the product

The product owners will enrich a story map with more information, based on feedback from various sources and through design sessions *(Patton, 2014).*

Some methods to add more information are:

- Use different colors to represent different levels of a story map, e.g., orange for goals, blue for features, green for epics, yellow for stories and purple for tasks
- Put wireframe next to the relevant area of a story map
- Use stickers like dots or stars to represent special notations:
    - o Marking out of scope features are important for shared understanding
    - o Identifying alternatives help to capture rich user experience and low-cost alternative solutions
    - o Identifying critical sequences or dependencies
- Use small stickers to capture notes, assumption, follow-ups or questions

When writing stories, strive to make sure that each story has as many of the **INVEST** attributes as possible:

- Independent. Each story should be independent of another, especially for stories that are being worked on during the same iteration, since dependencies between stories during the same iteration complicate planning and prioritization. Splitting the stories is a way to reduce or eliminate dependencies within an iteration.

- Negotiable. A story is negotiable, and the story is intended to be an 'invitation to a conversation' with the team(s) building it. The details associated with the story are worked out during this conversation.

- Valuable. The value associated with the story should be readily understood which is why the product owner plays such an important role in helping the team understand the 'why' and the 'what' of the story. The technical detail (the 'how') associated with each story is to be found in any task associated with that story, and the team determines the 'how' based on their understanding of the 'why' and the 'what'.

- Estimable. At the very least, the story needs to be clear enough for the team to do an initial estimate of the story's relative size. Common issues that can impede the team's ability to estimate a story include lack of domain knowledge (which is why the 'conversation' around the story is so important) and stories that are excessively large (in which case the story needs to be split into one or more smaller stories).

- Small. A story must be small enough to be completed during an iteration. Depending on team size, iteration length, and other factors, teams typically make stories small enough so that at least half a dozen can be completed during an iteration. Larger stories create problems for teams, and thus teams should seek ways to split stories into smaller parts.

- **T**estable. If a story is not testable, it is virtually impossible for the team, not to mention the product owner, to know when the story is 'done'. A classic anti-pattern is when a story contains imprecise language such as 'easy to use' (since there is no straightforward way to test ease of use). Therefore, acceptance criteria need to be written in such a way that the testing approach can readily be derived from them.

Story splitting exercise becomes mandatory when the team feels the need to decompose stories further to analyze, estimate, or fit into an iteration. If the story is too large or it requires more clarification given, it contains hidden characteristics. When considering how to split a story, keep the following guidelines in mind:

- Choose a pattern that results in one or more post-split stories that can be deprioritized or even eliminated. Suppose that applying one split pattern exposes low-value functionality, and another does not; this may be a sign that application of the latter split conceals waste (i.e., low-value work) inside the post-split stories. Apply the split pattern that makes it possible to deprioritize or eliminate work.

- Choose a pattern that results in similarly sized post-split stories. If the post-split stories are similarly sized, it makes prioritization easier *(Rogers, 2018)*.

Once the story splitting exercise is complete, the product owner can assess the size of the stories again, arrange stories to be equal in size and measurable for the team. The assessment exercise can be repeated with the team as many times as required; the whole purpose is to give the team properly sized stories to work on and avoid any delays in clarifications. A simple story will also be easy to understand, estimate, schedule into an iteration, and test.

The new generation of product owners is conscious of continuous learning through story mapping. For each product increment or release, you will need measures to observe whether the team produces

the outcomes as expected. Over time and with practice, product owners learn to develop and own the stories that prioritize the iterations to enhance products. Mapping the stories allows product owners to understand better the big picture of the product they are developing and prioritize the stories based on the inherent value they produce.

MVP - Myth or Reality

Often product owners focus too much on the Minimum Viable Product (MVP) at the outset of the initial iteration. In doing so, it constrains some of the benefits of the iterative approach. While the MVP can be a useful means of encouraging teams and stakeholders to understand and apply the concept of simplicity, what is more important is the incremental journey towards minimum sustainable delivery. The journey provides the opportunity for feedback and learning, and the potential to identify solutions that meet user needs in a simpler way than expected *(Yoxall, 2016)*.

The acronym, MVP, is increasingly becoming misused or used as a buzzword to justify any number of actions. Not only that the acronym is often misplaced with MPV, following the NPV (Net Present Value) acronym, but the MVP function is being misapplied. Here are three common MVP myths:

1. MVPs are delivering only the features an organization can afford. Meaning that the focus is on the approved budget and not on delivering value and testing the appetite of the customer. MVPs work around a fixed budget; however, the focus is the value being delivered, not the fixed budget.

2. MVPs with more features are better for the customer. The more features given to customers, the harder it will be to ask for feedback and test the features that do not work.

3. Failing MVPs mean failing products. The MVP can never fail. It is to test the market and your customers and get as much

feedback as possible early in the process. If anything, the MVP failing is a success story as you now understand what customers do not want.

The concept of creating an MVP before a full-scale product originates from the best practices of product development. This approach stipulates step-by-step product evolution keeping in mind user feedback. It also corresponds to the philosophy of 'ship early, repair later' supported by many notable minds including Reid Hoffman, founder of LinkedIn, as well as Eric Ries. It was Eric Ries who first introduced the MVP technique in his 'The Lean Startup'. Since that time, the developer community has become obsessed with this advanced mindset. In the meantime, obsession led to the emergence of widespread misunderstanding of what the MVP is meant for and what benefits it brings to startups, diminishing the value of the MVP concept and bringing a bad connotation to the acronym.

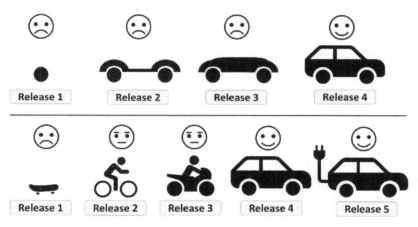

Figure 5.4: MVP Concept

A product can be called minimally viable if it has some features to be validated within the market and it brings the core value for early adopters. That is what most product owners have in mind when defining the features of an MVP. From the implementation viewpoint, MVP may be treated as a pioneer product version with raw functionality and features. It is not a first or fundamental layer of the cake, it

is just a piece of it, which you can give to customers to obtain their feedback. Most of the notable products, including Twitter or Instagram started their way as MVPs and have been gradually evolving into trendsetting startups. Meanwhile, new entrepreneurs may doubt the necessity and feasibility of this concept and prefer to skip the MVP stage. Such a decision may have an irreversible outcome, and your startup may end in disaster.

These are the characteristics of an MVP that the new generation of product owners should follow:

- **Goal**. The MVP is not to get a stripped-down product for cheap. Product owners need it to validate their opportunity hypothesis and get the green light for developing a full-fledged product. In other words, you essentially ask target customers whether they need your product or not. Though it is functionally-constrained and raw in the appearance, it is meant to deliver the core value and get feedback to move on.

- **Benefits**. What would have happened if the founders of Uber or Spotify had entered the market without a preliminary evaluation of their MVPs? It is more than likely that we would have not even known about their products. However, they made the right choice and leveraged the lean startup tactic, in which the MVP's role is fundamental. MVPs must be used to validate the benefits and value being delivered to customers.

- **Resources optimization**. Your idea might be brilliant in your head, but the market may reject it for various reasons like tough competition, or inadequate value proposition. As a result, tons of hours and money are spent on an unwanted product. The MVP gives you a chance to avoid this scenario and try out your opportunity hypothesis with actual customers. If the market accepts your bare-bones product, the chances of success with the fully-functional solution are quite high. If not, you avoid the risk of wasting time and money and

get an opportunity to shift focus or fix the value proposition of your startup.

- **Early customer acquisition**. MVP is a lean version of a product you are going to release to the market. Though it lacks some top-notch features and advanced functionality, it provides value to customers and hence acquires early adopters. Of course, the main goal of such an immature product release is to gather feedback to validate the value proposition. Nevertheless, it does not prevent you from starting to work with key startup metrics and make up a customer base.

- **Value proposition focus**. The last, but not least answer to the question 'why is minimum viable product important?' is the ultimate emphasis on the value you are going to deliver with your product. The MVP lets you understand the different problems your future customers need to solve. You can take advantage of using the value proposition canvas to get a graphical expression of customers' needs versus product offers and get feedback.

The key benefits of using the MVP approach include product owners that can create value for organizations, checking their product's vision with customers, optimizing people and resources to be spent on the product, and tailoring a product to enhance value.

An example of a business that started as a simple MVP is Airbnb. It started as a simple site launched by three founders who came up with the assumption that people wouldn't be able to find a place to stay during the Industrial Design Society of America Conference in San Francisco in 2007. So, they piled up all their beds in their small apartment and put up a simple ad about renting an air bed on a simple web page. Soon, they had three guests who wanted to share their apartment. Once they had proven that their idea was not a waste of time and money, they started looking at how to redesign the platform. Today, Airbnb has 150 million customers, four million listings, and is valued at $30 billion. It offers not only accommodation but also provides

customers with lists of restaurants and events in destination cities along with feedback and ratings.

In the end, the MVP is only a concept. Whether we call it the minimum viable product (MVP) or the minimum loveable product (MLP) as some product owners like to do, it helps the product owners launch new features and products and test them with the customers. The MVP only has enough features to satisfy early adopters and no more. The only purpose of the MVP is to create the most basic version of your product on which you can gather feedback and iterate from there later, with new features that customers will ask for. That is what 'minimum' is about. The important part is to determine that your product is viable and lovable, having good quality features, simple and sellable, to resonate with customers and attract them.

CHAPTER 6

ENABLE EFFECTIVE OWNERSHIP

"In a very real way, ownership is the essence of leadership.
When you are 'ridiculously in charge,'
then you own whatever happens in a company."
—Henry Cloud

Unfortunately, many organizations continue to treat product owners as glorified go-betweens, people who simply facilitate conversations between the team and management. It is a mistake to treat a product owner as a proxy. The product owner must be empowered to make critical decisions, no matter how unpopular.

In a large bank, Veena was a Director of Product Management who supported a large portfolio of retail, small business, commercial, and corporate products. *"In today's world, access to the product is crucial"* Veena told us in an interview. One of her key products was undergoing a major enhancement with a dedicated team doing the work. The value to a customer has always been the center of any new product release or enhancement. Providing customers with a solution rather than just a product is key to success. For Veena, the focus was on the ability to communicate to the customer directly about the value of the product, more educational than selling and product promotion, or pushing.

When Veena was assigned responsibility as a product owner for four large agile labs, management started by stating that they did not need any product management team in the lab as it would be enough to have the project manager act as the product owner. For the executive team, the project managers were equipped to play the role of the product owners. Neither of these was successful! Veena believed the product managers knew the customers the best. They, along with the sales folks, needed to be involved right through the agile journey.

Veena reflects that the Agile Labs were successful once they started the following:

- Product owners held interviews with customers asking what their pain points were, and if they would like to be involved in the product journey.

- Product owners created a customer journey mapping even before involving the team. The customer journey mapping included: vendors, customers, other stakeholders like compliance, risk, call center, etc.

- Product owners owned the product and worked with the team full time. They spoke for the customers as they received feedback from customers and other sources that regularly interacted with customers, for example, call centers, sales, and service centers.

For Veena, being an engaged product owner allowed her organization to have successful products.

Own it up, Product Owners!

The new generation of product owners means a generation of people empowered to own the products they are responsible for delivering. What does ownership mean? Accountability, decision making, and reliability. These three characteristics make the product owner an en-

tity of power in the organization focused on aligning strategic objectives with product features and conducting market analysis to support the customers.

Instead of ownership, product owners could: visit, borrow, or rent products. Historically in many organizations, product owners were visitors. A 'visitor' product owner works in a different functional department and would occasionally drop in to visit the functional groups that work on the part of the product, just like Veena did in the example above. The visitor product owner would oversee or watch what the team was doing, offer a few comments, provide some guidance or observations, and then leave. The visitor product owner is not around to support the team while they do their work on the product, provide guidance to the product, or to clear roadblocks for the team. They are just visiting.

The 'borrower' product owner would own the product for just a short time. This is often seen in organizations where project managers or business analysts fill the role of a product owner. The project manager or business analyst would be someone temporarily assigned to manage a product or portfolio of products and would borrow the product to enhance the product by adding features. Once the features are delivered, the project manager or business analyst turn the product over to operations for them to manage the product and maintain it. The project manager or business analyst is just trying to ensure the product will meet quality standards and is completed within the budget and on schedule. Once the product is done and delivered, the project manager or business analyst has no further interest in the product. The product which is temporarily borrowed and developed sometimes lacks the long-term vision to guide future product enhancements.

The 'renter' product owner, on the other hand, has a longer-term commitment to a product than the borrower product owner. The renter product owner is going to be involved with the product for a year or two but ultimately sees the product as a stepping-stone to

another job or opportunity. The renter product owner uses the product to help them advance their objectives, and then they move on. A renter product owner may add some cosmetic changes to the product, but they are not going to resolve any long-term issues with the product. A renter product owner is not going to invest in the product for the long-term; they are just interested in the short-term objectives of the products.

Ownership of a product means that as a product owner, you are developing a long-term relationship with the product. An owner is looking at the product to be successful both in the short and the long-term aspects and is willing to make investments in the product to help sustain the growth of the product over multiple years.

Attribute	Visitor	Borrower	Renter	Owner
Time	Very short	Short	Medium	Long
Investment	Very low	Very low	Medium	High
Passion	Very low	Low	Medium	High

Table 6.1: Types of Product Ownership

Doug needs to visit a friend about 50 kilometers away in a remote community where there is no access to public transit. For this example, the product is the vehicle that can take Doug from his home to visit his friend. Which vehicle (product) Doug uses for the trip will define the type of product owner Doug is:

- ***Visitor.** As a visitor, Doug would hire a taxicab or Uber to visit his friend. Doug would do nothing to improve the car and may even leave some garbage in the car.*
- ***Borrower.** Doug borrows his neighbor's car to drive to his friend. Doug makes sure the gas tank is full when he returns the car and all the garbage is removed.*

- **Renter.** *Doug rents the car from the rental car agency to drive to his friend. Doug also uses the car to pick up some items before returning it to the rental agency with a full tank of gas and on time.*
- **Owner.** *Doug buys a car for the trip to drive to his friend. Doug takes care of the car, cleans it, pays for insurance, and fills its tank regularly. Doug can now visit his friend anytime.*

The new generation of product owners must have five characteristics or feelings specific to product ownership, also called the 5Ps:

- **Pride.** A product owner has the pride of ownership. You are proud to have your name associated with the product and are satisfied with the effort you have put into the product to develop and enhance it.

- **Power.** As a product owner, you have the authority to make decisions about the product that you own. You can add features to grow the product and respond to customer needs and feedback.

- **Promotion.** As a product owner, you can make decisions on how to market and sell your products, allowing you to feel the joy of success and disappointment of failure for the products you own.

- **Protection.** As a product owner, you care and nurture the products for which you are accountable, adding for more features to develop them. You are protecting your products by the way you respond to customer's feedback to ensure that the product would benefit from the feedback in continuous improvement releases.

- **Passion.** As a product owner, passion will give you the incentive to build your product. Bringing the energy through your passion will inspire all the stakeholders who want to join you on your product journey.

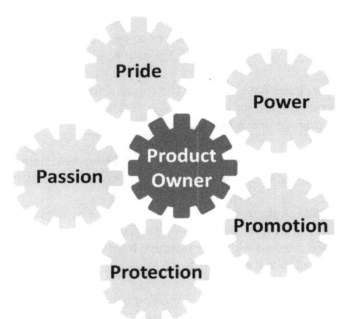

Figure 6.1: 5Ps of Product Ownership

The new generation of product owners requires all the ownership skills and characteristics to add value to the organization. They need to have a pride of ownership, have the authority to act in the best interest of the product, ensure the product is successful, and nurture the product through the product life cycle, allowing the product to evolve and transform according to the needs of the customers over a long time.

Who is the Product Owner?

Organizations have transformed the workplace in recent years to find better ways to work in an environment challenged by innovation and rapid growth. The product owners are themselves a product. They are the result of a new way of working, known as the agile way of working. This new concept allows the team to get closer to the customer they deliver the product for and find ways of releasing benefits

to the customer as often as they can. The product owner is the role of making the connection with the most important stakeholder, the customer, of bringing the team together to deliver valuable products and ultimately of aligning the organization's objectives to the needs of the customer. There are two key characteristics of the role of product owner:

- Product owners revolve around products and products grow organizations. To make an organization successful, it is about the outcome, not the role or job title.

- Product owners are inspired by products to develop an appropriate team culture, thus dictating the speed of growth in any organization; and to discuss the need for a strategy, ensuring there is an alignment with the organization's strategy for many years. The key to strategic alignment is to ensure the products that the organization invests in deliver benefits that are linked to strategic goals.

Traditionally, product owners are in the marketing department due to their customer experience responsibility, listening to the voice of the customer, and developing a plan using the 4Ps of marketing: **price**, **promotion**, **place**, and **product**. Based on direct feedback from customers, the marketing department would develop a list of features that they would like to add to the product and work with other departments in their organization to make it happen. In other cases, the product owner is in the sales department as they would know best what product features customers purchase. The sales department's focus is on revenue objectives, which does not lead to long-term product sustainability. Product owners can also come from the engineering or technology departments, who are responsible for the design and development of the product. They rely mostly on sales and marketing to figure out how to sell the product, whether there is a market for the product, or not. In project-based organizations, the project sponsor could be the product owner as the project sponsor has the responsibility to ensure that the product realizes the benefits for the organization.

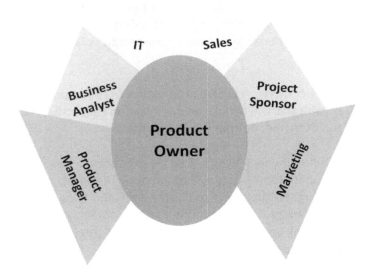

Figure 6.2: Product Owner Roles

Today's organizations are moving to flatter structures creating cross-functional teams or self-managing teams. With a flatter organization, it is easier to create teams with product skills in different areas lead by product owners. As a result, the team is responsible for the success of the product, delivering value to customers, obtaining feedback from customers, and enhancing the product to meet customers' needs.

Some organizations, from software development to financial services, health, and even governmental institutions, want to be agile and are establishing product owner positions as a standard role. The problem is that the role gets anchored to the Scrum definition of product owner, which may not be appropriate for the product or the organization. On the other hand, some of these organizations are just positioning the product owner as a role with no accountability for the product being developed. The new generation of product owners must go beyond Scrum, Kanban, Extreme programming (XP), or any

other framework to put the focus back on customer value delivery and organizational growth.

For organizations to successfully deliver strategy, they need to develop new products and enhance current products to achieve their strategic goals. To have sustained delivery, organizations need to have full-time new generation product owners that can focus on products to ensure they are delivering value to customers.

Product Owners Make It Happen!

As mentioned in Chapter 1, organizations deliver their strategy through products. Products are and should be linked to the strategic goals of the organization. Executing the strategic goals is the responsibility of the product owner, with one major outcome of delivering value. As such, product owners need to commission teams to develop and enhance their products.

The relationship between a product and a delivery method is critical. A product cannot exist without delivery mechanisms such as iterations, sprints, or project phases. The product development is known to rely on a delivery team that is brought together to deliver the features of the product. Without it, there will be no structure in the process, and the task would take much longer to complete.

The team should use a five-phase approach to deliver the product:

1. **Sprint planning**. Together with the product owner, the team identifies the prioritized stories to be included in the next iteration. The product owner should ensure the team has the required skills and people to complete the selected stories.

2. **Define**. The team develops the approach to deliver the stories, defining the details of the tasks that need to be completed. The product owner continues to support the team by providing guidance and sharing their vision for the product.

3. **Build**. The team builds the product and ensures the acceptance criteria are met. The product owner must be available to support the team's clear roadblocks and issues as they occur.

4. **Release**. The product owner decides whether the product is releasable based on its defined specifications and value-add for the customers.

5. **Product backlog**. The product owner and the team review the backlog and make adjustments based on lessons continuously learned from every release and feedback received from the customer.

Figure 6.3: Agile Product Life Cycle

As we discussed in Chapters 2 and 5, agility is an important characteristic of the new generation of product owners. In the case of product development, using an iterative approach to deliver a few features quickly is important. A product owner will have a team to support them. The team, in some cases, will have business analysts work-

ing full-time or part-time depending on the size of the product back-log to support the product owner with writing epics and user stories, as well as acceptance criteria. Product owners need to discuss with the team the appropriateness of using an adaptive or an iterative approach to develop the product. It is critical to have the appropriate method to create the product backlog and its purpose of continually adding features to it to enhance the marketability of the product.

The team should be turning the product over to the product owner so the product can be marketed, sold, and shipped to customers. Change management and product adoption is also the role of the product owner and the team. Ongoing maintenance and support of the product—to keep the product up to the standards—will also be the responsibility of the team, most of the maintenance and support activities translating into small releases. And finally, at the end of the iteration, the product owner needs to ensure the team celebrates their accomplishments.

In Chapter 4, we talked about the need to lead the team through any changes required to deliver or support the product. The product owner needs to create a team culture that fits with the organizational culture and has the following characteristics:

- The team must be singularly focused on the delivery value to customers through product increments.
- The team must ensure to reduce waste at every stage, meaning to prioritize the value features and leave the non-value ones aside.
- The team must always listen to feedback from customers and use the feedback to inform the direction of the product.
- The team must work together and rely on each other's expertise to estimate and prioritize the most valuable features.

Every organization should have a goal to build a well-respected brand, a company culture, and an amazing team around awesome products. Long-term success comes with a strong product pipeline.

Here are the four strategic steps Movable Ink used to build a great product-focused organization *(Gasca, 2015)*:

1. Create a strong, clear, and flexible roadmap with three levels:
   - **Short-term**. Focused on assessing the current demands and priorities and address quick wins.
   - **Mid-term**. Prioritize the second horizon features of the product to evolve current demands and ensure delivery for any short-term priorities that have not been delivered.
   - **Long-term**. Create a vision, the 'north star', for your product to guide product development decisions.

2. Conduct user research and product discovery by constantly validating the product plans with customers. The research will recognize the differences between new and repeat customers and their changing behaviors in time. It will also make the team constantly ask the following questions:
   - 'What problem are we solving?'
   - 'For whom are we solving the problem?'
   - 'How does solving the problem fundamentally move our business forward?'
   - 'Does this fit into the long-term strategy?'

3. Test, measure, and understand product ideas that could build potential value. Teams create early versions of the product with only the most viable features that are put in the hands of trusted customers. Feedback is gathered quickly to make the adjustments and understand why and where the product failed to deliver value.

4. Communicate regularly and transparently internally and externally. All organization members have access to communication, while customers are kept in the loop with changes coming or being made. This will ease the experience of both employees interested in the business developments of the

organization as well as customers learning how to use the new features of the product.

The new generation of product owners must know how to build and work with the team to deliver products using iterations.

The Circle of Trust

There is one key enabler of effective product ownership. Trust.

Open communication and an environment of sharing common goals build a team surrounded by trust. The product owner is more than often the glue of the team. The relationship between the product owner and the team is a relationship of reciprocal trust. The team trusts that the product owner understands the product needs and can prioritize the features based on that experience. The product owner trusts that the team can help in building quality features and delivering them in the promised timeframe. Trust is important outside the team as well, in the relationship between the product owner and the customer or other stakeholders. For that, the product owner demonstrates empathy and understands everyone's perspectives, analyzing and prioritizing their gains and pains.

In their book, *Trust and Betrayal in the Workplace*, Dennis Reina and Michelle Reina present three elements of trust: the trust of capability, the trust of character, and the trust of communication *(Riena, 2015)*. This is a good model to look at how product owners can build trust.

- **Trust of capability**. Product owners need to show they trust the capability of the team, understand the skills and abilities of their team members and match tasks that have to be done to the skills of team members, and appropriately delegating work to team members. Delegation, including delegating decisions to the team, helps build trust between the team and the product owner. If a team member does not have the skills to do the task, a product owner can find ways for the team

member to gain the skills which allow them to successfully complete the assigned tasks.

- **Trust of character**. Trust starts with the product owner who needs to build trust with all product stakeholders to be successful. One of the easiest ways to build trust with others is to say what you are going to do and do it. Trust is built by setting expectations, establishing boundaries, while ensuring that the expectations are met, and boundaries are held. Product owners can also build trust, being consistent with their emotions, and with rewards and recognition.

- **Trust of communication**. Product owners need to communicate with the team what is expected of them. Product owners need to communicate with customers about the product value, receiving feedback, and actions taken based on customer feedback. It is one thing to communicate, and another to communicate in a way to build trust. To communicate to build trust requires sharing information, telling the truth, admit when mistakes have been made, maintain confidentiality and be a good listener.

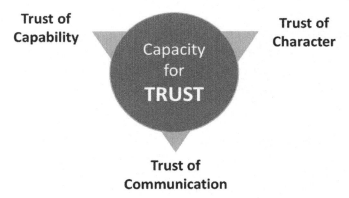

Figure 6.4: Capacity for Trust

The Reina model provides a good way to build trust, but you need to continue to build trust every day. Trust is one of the things that are

easier to break than to build. It is so easy to make a simple mistake to say something wrong that will cause the trust to be broken or put into question. For product owners, it is necessary to focus on these three elements and continually work to build the capabilities of the team, your character, and to communicate and communicate to build trust.

In the Battle of Trafalgar, Admiral Nelson leads the English fleet into the battle against the joint fleets of the French and Spanish that outnumbered the English fleet. To defeat the Spanish and French fleets, Nelson came up with a radically different strategy. Instead of having the English ships lined up opposite the Franco-Spanish ships and fire cannons at each other, Nelson's strategy was to have the English ships sail through the enemy line. For this strategy to work, Nelson needed the English ship captains to trust him as he trusted the captains of each of the English ships. Nelson made sure that each of his captains could command their ship and to do what was required of them to implement his strategy. Nelson worked hard on himself as well, to build consistent messages and to ensure the captains knew what was expected of them. Nelson communicated the strategy to the captains showing that he trusted them and that they would keep the battle plans secret. Also, they had to know what to do, after all, in 1805, there were no text messages to resolve issues. History shows that Nelson's strategy worked, and the English won the Battle of Trafalgar. In part, this was due to Nelson's brilliant strategy, but one cannot discount it was Nelson's ability to communicate the strategy and to earn the trust of the English captains who, in return trusted Nelson to have a winning strategy (McChrystal, 2015).

The new generation of product owners is a generation of Nelsons. Empowering the team members and entrusting them to deliver on the jointly defined strategy will be a recipe for just in time product delivery.

VALUE SUSTAINED DELIVERY

*"What the customer buys and considers value is never a product.
It is always utility, that is, what a product
or service does for the customer."*
–Peter Drucker

The higher the average customer's lifetime value, the more you can spend to attract a new customer, making it possible to spread the word about your offer in new ways. Having a high lifetime value even allows you to lose money on the first sale. Guthy-Renker sells a typical acne treatment called Proactiv using long-form expensive television infomercials. Proactiv is spending millions to produce and air the infomercials, hiring popular or celebrity endorsers. At first glance, it does not make any sense: the first sale is for a very low price of $20. One would think that Proactiv does not make money when a customer purchases Proactiv. However, the customers are not just buying a single bottle of cream, they are signing up to receive a bottle every month in exchange for a recurring payment.

The lifetime value of each new Proactiv customer is so high, that it does not matter to Guthy-Renker that there is no profit margin on the initial sale, the company makes a ton of money using expensive advertising, even if some customers do not continue with the program. The first sale is sometimes called a 'loss leader', meaning an

enticing offer intended to establish a relationship with a new customer *(Kauffman, 2012)*.

Reliable and Sustainable: The Magic Product

Long term value can come from different ways of combining and prioritizing the value creation and value delivery streams. The value creation of a product like Proactiv is in the competitive advantage of its service strategy of delivering a unique value proposition. Once the product is purchased, the organization's value is created by maintaining a recurrent offer, while customers benefit from the convenience of the service. The small hooks that keep customers engaged and willing to buy repeatedly are the key to business growth.

With value-driven product ownership, productive teams can quickly respond to customer feedback and create product iterations with sustained results. Sustainability empowers organizations to invest, experiment, grow and thrive over time. Just focusing on delivering value to the customer without considering the cost impacts to the organization often results in high costs and a business model that is not sustainable. On the other hand, just focusing on internal processes to ensure optimal efficiency to create products at the lowest possible cost does not ensure delivering value to customers. As a product owner, to build a magic product, you need a balance between the value creation focused on quality and value delivery focused on consumerism to keep the product alive.

Some time ago, a Japanese home-appliance company was trying to develop a coffee percolator. Executives were asking, "Should it be a General Electric-type machine? Should it be the drip-type of the kind Philips makes? Larger? Smaller?" the product owner urged them to ask a different question: 'Why do people drink coffee?' The answer came back: good taste. After further research, the company found that this 'good taste' had a few critical components: water quality, coffee-grain distribution, the time elapsed between grinding and brewing. Certain things mattered more than others. That got the

company thinking differently about the percolator's essential features. Suddenly, it had to have a built-in de-chlorinator and, of course, a built-in grinder. If you pay attention only to your competitors, you compete only on the features that they, perhaps wrongly, consider important. If you focus on the fact that the new GE machine brews coffee in ten minutes, you will work feverishly to make a machine that brews it in seven. Never mind that the customers are nearly indifferent.

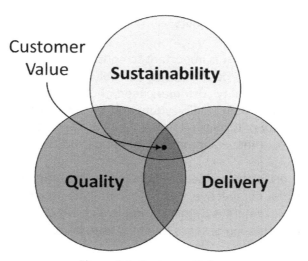

Figure 7.1: Customer Value

Unless you step back and ask, 'What are the customer's fundamental needs, and what is this product really about?' you may find delivering a product that no one needs. You will produce an ultra-low-cost piano that no one wants to buy, or a percolator that can brew a pot of undrinkable coffee almost instantaneously, or a forklift that piles up a record number of boxes but does not allow operators to see directly in front of themselves *(Golub, 2000)*.

Modern quality has its foundation in Japan manufacturing since the 1950s. The principles of modern quality have been continuously reinvented:

- **Customer satisfaction**. Quality is defined by the customer and is based on conformance to requirements and fitness to use.
- **Prevention over inspection**. Quality is planned, designed, and built-in, not inspected out, which results in waste reduction.
- **Continuous improvement**. Use Deming's Plan-do-check-act cycle or the iteration approach discussed in Chapter 5.
- **Management responsibility**. Everyone in the organization is responsible for quality.

As a product owner, it is important to consider these four principles as you create your product. Quality and value are interrelated. If you do not have the quality customers need, then you are not delivering value. If you have high quality, your customers will not pay the price. The four quality principles reinforce the need for customer feedback and to use an iterative approach to develop products.

One of the principles of modern quality is continuous improvement. From a process perspective, the most commonly used model for continuous improvement is Deming's simple Plan-Do-Check-Act (PDCA). A simple walkthrough of these four steps can bring improvements to any process.

1. **Plan.** The focus is on defining the problem and coming up with a solution. This includes defining a team and estimating a timeline.

2. **Do**. This step is about the execution of the plan to implement the solution identified. This is an opportunity to experiment and see whether it works, document the steps taken, and collect feedback.

3. **Check**. This step is about reviewing the results of the implemented solution and comparing them to the original plan. If the plan was not successful, the team could go back to the

first step (planning) while considering the learning experience. If the solution was successful, then the team can focus on the next step.

4. **Act**. This step is about implementing the solution fully, as a new baseline against which the team will continue to measure for future improvements. In continuous improvement, every new addition becomes a new baseline for the next.

Traditionally, product owners break down their delivery model in production terms of three steps:
1. Design the product;
2. Make the product; and
3. See the product.

For product owners in Industry 3.0, working on cost-cutting initiatives, the focus is on expense rationalization. As a new generation of product owners working in Industry 4.0, delivering a compelling value proposition, it makes more sense to divide up the operational model into customer-oriented steps:
1. Choose the value;
2. Provide the value; and
3. Communicate the value to customers.

This is the value delivery model that will allow you to integrate the various roles and approaches in all three customer-oriented steps. Then you can measure if the chosen value model pervades every layer of your organization and becomes sustainable. The winning strategy is the one that implements the value proposition to the customer, not the one whose proposition was the most appealing for the organization. If the organization takes the value model seriously, the product owners can ask teams to contribute to the measure of value that was previously chosen. This sometimes results in sacrificing the cost efficiency approaches in favor of value proposition that aims for organizational objectives: adding the right type of value for the right customer segments.

The new generation of product owners must build products that are reliable and sustainable, with the ability to exist and improve constantly.

IKEA has a dedicated team for sustainable product development. The team is responsible for developing the range of home furnishing products. Business areas have dedicated sustainability leaders, supported by a central group of sustainability specialists. They are responsible for leading and supporting the sustainability work within product development and supply chain. Product developers, technicians, and other key internal stakeholders are invited to take part in training modules on waste and innovation. IKEA even introduced a sustainability product scorecard to help the organization move toward more sustainable product development. The 11 criteria on the scorecard are focused on the sustainability profile throughout the product life cycle. These sustainable measures are making IKEA products more desired and increase the productivity of the organization.

It feels magical when some products sell without any effort, while others remain on the physical or virtual shelves. IKEA is an example of an organization whose products continue to sell. Still very much relying on the physical stores, IKEA builds an entire experience on top of the products they sell. Their showcasing floors are built to make the IKEA walk to the store an entire experience. From the daycare services to their own restaurant, to the snack bar and resting areas, customers enjoy the shopping experience. The value of visiting the store resides not only in the products offered, but the entire customer experience.

Value is defined by productivity and growth levels, and it is measured by customer satisfaction and sustained support. Creating value is everybody's responsibility in organizations, combined with a constant approach to continuous improvement. Customer feedback allows the organization to learn about changing behaviors and needs. If organizations understand customers who have the right to change their needs and desires, they will be able to build sustainable products. IKEA is again an example of such an organization, its product

catalogs showing continuously new products being introduced, old-time products being offered at regular discounts, and most desired items being highlighted based on feedback from customers.

Value Comes in Streams

Organizations need to identify the streams or flows of materials or information that produce value for customers. A value stream is a series of steps that occur to provide the product or service customers need. Identifying and mapping these value streams in intelligible sequences is called value stream mapping (VSM). This process provides a structured visualization of the key steps and the data required to proactively make improvements to the entire process, not just a portion of it. *"Value stream maps offer a holistic view of how workflows through entire systems" (Martin, 2014).*

Value stream mapping has been growing in popularity in recent years, and it is still a new tool for business and process efficiency. The biggest reason for its existence is the increased complexity in organizations' flow. VSM can help improve the flow by reducing wait times and eliminating waste from removing steps that add no value. This method will help create a current view of the organization's process and focus on items that can be changed to address specific objectives. Like any other tool, VSM is focused on decreasing the cost of the process and increasing the value it produces, therefore minimizing the waste in the flow.

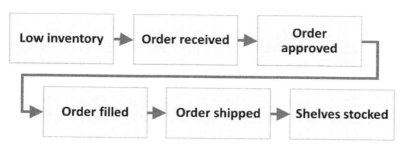

Figure 7.2: Simplified Value Stream

A value stream includes all activities required to transform customer requests into a delivered product. It is basically the combination of value creation and value delivery processes to satisfy the customer's needs. That is why a value stream needs to be as nimble and efficient as possible, to produce value fast and solicit customer feedback. If we look at the entire process, it looks like there are a lot of steps for a simple product restocking process. That is why it is so important for organizations to understand all the steps through the delivery of the result to the customer. Monitoring the value streams periodically is critical for ensuring that there are no recent delays or anything that can be improved as a result of recent innovations.

Toyota was the first big manufacturing organization examining its entire value stream regularly. By doing this, the automaker was able to have small, incremental improvements to their process. Toyota engineers make over one million improvements to their TPS each year (*Kauffman, 2012*). As a result of these reviews and thorough examinations, Toyota has been able to improve the speed, consistency, and reliability of its products, boosting at some point the company's reputation for high-quality products.

With the Lean movement and the need to define dependencies between value streams, the mapping method developed by Toyota continued to evolve the value stream mapping method. Building a VSM requires several steps:

1. **Define the focus**. Where in the larger process do you want to deliver increased value.

2. **VSM team selection**. Create a team with diverse skills from all levels in the organization, including the product owner.

3. **Go to Gemba**. Gemba is the Japanese word for 'walk the place', which is used to get the team as close to the customer as possible.

4. **Define the basic value stream**. Create the starting point and the basics of the VSM to create a background for further discussions.

5. **Team mapping activity**. Use the diversity of the team to create maps that can be shared with everyone, sparking collaborative discussions.

6. **Develop a current state value stream map**. From the basic VSM completed in step four, the team will add more detail processes and data, including current cycle times, lead times, uptimes, takt times, and service level agreements (SLAs).

7. **Develop target state value stream map**. The target state represents a clear, measurable target goal to be achieved.

8. **Develop future state value stream map**. The future state VSM identifies the hot points, bottlenecks, strengths, and weaknesses of the process and identifies an implementation plan with 30, 60, and 90-day objectives.

To identify the challenges and delays in a value stream, some lean experts will start with current state data and look for hot points, bottlenecks or issues that can be easily resolved. It applies the method of low hanging fruit and from there prioritizes changes to processes. Others will start with the end in mind, the target state, and work back until the total time is reduced to meet the target time.

For example, you are the product owner for a specialized brand of coffee beans. You have received feedback from customers that the product is not available in retail stores for them to purchase. The feedback constantly says that they love the fresh product and the taste but are frustrated by going to stores and finding the coffee is sold out. Your product is sold in specialized coffee stores that are independently owned. Each store is responsible for monitoring its inventory. Packages need to meet a variety of requirements to be on

the shelves. The process of supplying merchandise in the store is as follows:

- Low inventory triggers store to place order
- Order is received, reviewed
- Internal approval process
- Order is filled
- Order is shipped
- Store receives order and place on shelves

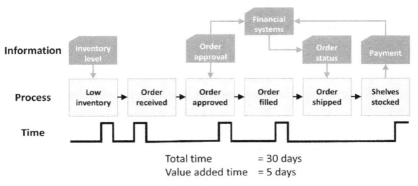

Total time = 30 days
Value added time = 5 days

Figure 7.3: Current State Value Stream Map

Looking at this on the value map, the order takes a total time of 30 days to complete, and there are several options that slow down the process. Only five days of the total time of 30 days is an actual value-add to the process. The store cannot track inventory and only know that they have no coffee beans only when a customer asks. The approval process of the order takes a long time, with very few orders rejected.

As a product owner, you could work with your organization to drop the approval step in the process, saving a week of time. You could also look at a way to interface with the store's point of sale terminals allow you to monitor the inventory levels and send coffee beans when required (the Walmart approach). With this, the new process would look like:

- Order reviewed when inventory is lower
- Order is filled
- Order is shipped
- Store receives order and place on shelves

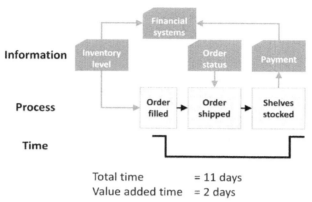

Total time = 11 days
Value added time = 2 days

Figure 7.4: Target State Value Stream Map

The target process takes a total time of 11 days, reducing wait time by 19 days, while the value-added time is reduced to two days.

Feedback is Gold

Throughout the product life cycle, it is important to get feedback continuously, and there are certain instances during the product life cycle where product owners must obtain feedback. These instances are:

- Backlog Prioritization
- Product Review
- Product Acceptance
- Team Retrospective

As a new generation of product owners, you must ensure that you are addressing customers' most critical problems to deliver the maximum value. To do this, you need to understand what the customer

values and that your user stories have the potential to solve the customer problems. To get this insight, you need to get feedback from customers as you prioritize and select user stories from the backlog to put into a product iteration. The customer feedback at this point can be obtained through meetings, surveys, focus groups, observations, and mockup reviews. As a product owner, it is important to ensure that you hear what the customers need, not what they want, and not what you think they need.

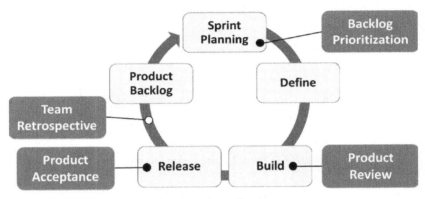

Figure 7.5: Formal Feedback Instances

During product development, product owners need to check with customers to ensure that the value that was expected will be delivered when the iteration is completed. While working on the product iteration, the team should schedule regular times to meet with customers to review the work. It is during these reviews that customers can provide critical feedback on the 'fitness of use' for features and if they will deliver the expected value.

During review meetings, the customer can view prototypes, test certain features in a test environment, or see a demonstration of features. No matter which approach is used, this should be done in a way where customer's feedback can be collected either directly from their experience or indirectly through observation. The objective of these review meetings is to ensure the customer sees value in the product and can get the benefits from the product that was originally

anticipated. If during the reviews the customer is not getting the value that is expected or is struggling with certain features, then the design of the product or the implementation of the features can be changed to improve the customer experience. Doing this early in the iteration will minimize waste for not having to launch a product that does not meet the customers' needs. It will also build knowledge about how to position the product in the marketplace to be successful and provide insights to improve the development of future features. The other key benefit of regular product reviews is that it helps ensure the product will be accepted by customers when the iteration is completed.

In some cases, a formal customer or product owner's acceptance of the product must be obtained before it is launched. The acceptance may be presented in the form of a sign-off, especially when there is a legal contract involved. In this case, it is important that at the start of the product iteration you obtain clear acceptance criteria; during the development of the product you ensure that you measure the acceptance criteria, and you share the results with the customer during the regular review meetings. By doing this, the customer will accept the product at the end of the iteration, knowing that the product is going to meet the acceptance criteria. In other cases, acceptance of the product is determined by the marketplace by answering the question: Are customers buying your product? If the answer is yes, then customers accept your product. If the answer is no, then it means the customers do not see value in your product. In this case, many organizations will use focus groups or pilots to test a product's sellability index, before they do a full-scale launch of the product.

As we discussed in Chapter 5, it is part of product growth to deliver first an MVP, and if it is not accepted by customers, then take time to learn and make the necessary changes. As a product owner, it is important that you understand the process of accepting your product by the customer and the organization, and that you plan for this acceptance throughout the product development iteration.

The fourth formal feedback channel to obtain feedback are retrospectives with the customer and the team. A retrospective is an opportunity to gather feedback on how well you and the team have been working and identify ways for future improvements. This type of session is also called lessons learned. The idea of a retrospective is to collect information in a structured way to allow you to determine how to improve your process going forward into the next phase or iteration for your product development. A retrospective meeting generally has five steps:

1. Set the stage for why the meeting is occurring;
2. Gather data from the attendees;
3. Generate insights from the data that has been gathered;
4. Determine the actions to be taken to improve the process; and
5. Wrap-up the meeting.

There are several techniques that can be used to gather data during retrospective meetings. Some of the common techniques include:

- **What went well, what should be done better**. Ask each attendee to reflect on what was done well in the iteration and what can be improved for the next iteration.
- **Stop-start-continuing**. Ask each attendee to respond to what should the team stop doing, continue doing, and start to do.

- **Mad, sad, glad.** Ask each attendee to say what they are mad about since the last retrospective, what they are sad about, and what they are glad about.

- **Draw me a picture**. This is a nonverbal approach where the attendees draw a picture of how they feel about the iteration.

- **Six hats of thinking**. Use De Bono's 6 Thinking Hats (white for facts, blacks for cautions, red for feelings, blue for process, yellow for benefits, and green for creativity) to structure

ways to discuss the team's observations on the iteration using one hat at a time.

Whichever technique is used, it is important that the team feels they can share what they are thinking safely. Also, using a technique that will allow the team to generate insight into their performance will create action items and will allow the team to improve their performance.

Getting feedback is gold! As a product owner, getting feedback in a structured way will increase gaining customer acceptance. With customer acceptance as you are delivering value, you get the ultimate gold payoff, and the customer will pay and use your product. However, there is even more important gold. Feedback will show you ways to see how you can deliver additional value to the customer, thus creating sustainable value for your customers.

It's not the End, It's the Beginning

Once the product iteration is complete, the product is selling, and customers are providing valid feedback; the team can declare themselves satisfied. However, the work is not complete. Building a sustainable and competitive product means that the team needs to continue to make small changes to improve the offer. Continuous augmentation is the process of using the iterative approach to create new value to the existing product. It can be a simple process of start-stop-continue that validates core assumptions defined at the beginning of product development. The intent is to start adding features that increment the product, continue doing what works for the customer, and stop doing what does not.

The MVP concept is a challenge given its purpose of releasing a product only with the necessary features to attract enough customers and get their feedback. The MVP is just the beginning of the journey. The product must be continuously enhanced to ensure that customers receive value. As mentioned in Chapter 1, organizations face three key challenges today: diversity, technology, and business models. If your

product continues to evolve, then your competitors will take advantage of the changes in the world and technology and attract your customers.

There are two major elements in the product journey that make a difference: feedback from customers and continuous replenishment of the product backlog. In this chapter, there is a focus on collecting customer feedback. As a product owner, you need to collect feedback from customers to build additional features that generate more value. However, customers are not the only source of feedback. As a product owner, you need to get input from a variety of sources including your team, your suppliers, what your competitors are doing (mysterious shopper method), and especially what they are not doing and why. You also need to look further afield to see what other trends are happening in the world.

ANZ Bank in Australia started its digital transformation in early 2015, investing almost US$300M into this initiative. Then it followed up with an innovation lab in Singapore the following year. The approach the Australian bank took was to observe the behavior of Fintechs (financial technology organizations, often startups) and follow their innovation partners. The bank also made a couple of partnerships with Fintechs, using them as an opportunity for partnership in innovative technology, such as machine learning. "Banks, too, have to adapt 'old ways of working' when collaborating with start-ups," said Iyer. Iyer said ANZ has partnered with fintech start-ups to improve its businesses, and there are opportunities to do more using technology such as artificial intelligence and blockchain technology (Lee, 2019).

Learning from smaller, more nimble organizations has become a priority for large businesses as they see the value in experimenting and trying new things. The smaller they are, the better organizations can adapt to changes and create value sooner. It all comes down to having a backlog of features that can be implemented faster, producing results and value to customers, while supplying new features fast enough for the teams to work on.

Regularly or once a product iteration is nearing the end, the product backlog needs to be reviewed and prioritized. This is not a job for the product owner alone. The prioritization should include a diverse group of people who can ensure that the most valuable features in the backlog have the top priority. Once the features have been prioritized you need to divide them up into iterations. There are several criteria involved in creating an iteration. The most important for the new generation of product owners is to ensure that each iteration is an MVP of features being built on top of the last iteration. Iterations need to be small and flexible to allow experimentation and focused feedback.

Continuous improvement was introduced as a need to add features to products and build iterations. Kaizen is the practice of continuous improvement and was developed to improve Japanese manufacturing processes by lowering costs and improving quality. Kaizen translates to 'change for the better', a simple concept that is now used by companies all over the world at the individual, team, and organizational levels. The concept introduces four major interrelated categories that contribute to continuous improvement, building quality, and reducing waste:

- **Commitment**. The organization sets shared goals that are well understood by everyone. Through commitment, the product is developed to be more competitive over time and maintain an advantage in the industry.

- **Strategy**. The vision and mission of the organization are developed to keep the focus on improving the product regularly while focusing on value generated priorities.

- **Process**. Through process mapping and analysis, there is a continuous focus on incremental augmentation of features and capabilities of the product.

- **Performance**. Once the purpose of the product is defined, measurement policies are established. Results are mapped

against initial objectives, and action plans are developed for any gaps in product capabilities.

Figure 7.6: Continuous Improvement (Kaizen Method)

Quality is always the highest priority for Kaizen. However, quality does not refer to the finished product, but to all processes and standards required to create a product. Quality will pertain to all phases of product development, from design and development to implementation, sales, and services. Quality represents both the purpose and method of the product development cycle.

Kaizen has developed into a philosophy that educates employees on how to think differently about the work at all levels of the organization. The consistent application of Kaizen as an action plan that creates long-term value by building a culture of continuous improvement engages employees to suggest and implement improvements in organizations. Talents and diversification are a powerful engine for continuous improvement. The mechanism for collecting the ideas for improvement is also key; employees being offered a multitude of

channels to express and validate their feedback. The benefits of Kaizen include:

- **Capital Investments.** By investing in smaller, incremental changes, the organization does not need to supply significant capital people and resources. The changes can be done at a low cost and can generate a large impact.

- **Engaged workplace.** By encouraging everyone in the organization to contribute with ideas for improvement, they become more engaged and committed.

- **Long-term sustainability.** Each small change and improvement is built on previous ones, creating a value-add snowball effect.

- **Visual management.** By creating an environment where product development processes and tools are visible, opportunities for improvement are noticed right away.

Siemens Oostkamp applied Kaizen for their production plant. The results were very satisfactory. They were able to reduce the cost of inventory by 30%. Lead time for their coils went from 12 days to six days. The number of product types was reduced by 33%, and storage area was reduced by 10%. On top of that, employees became problem-solvers and fixed problems to products right away compared to before when it took them days to find a problem. The numbers did not show a happier, more fulfilled workforce who enjoys coming to work, but translated to fewer sick days, less employee turnover and better safety (Allred, 2019).

Product owners need to deal with the many critical touchpoints when their customers interact with products, on their way to purchase a product and post-purchase support. A routine service event, such as product query, may not result in a customer until months after as a 'product question.' As a new generation of product owners, being able to manage the entire customer experience through external and

internal interactions will give you enormous rewards: increased revenues, greater employee satisfaction, enhanced customer delight, and reduced waste. You will also find effective ways to collaborate across functions and levels for the benefit of the customer, not just for your organization.

EXCEL AS PRODUCT OWNERS

*"There are no secrets to success.
It is the result of preparation, hard work,
and learning from failure."*
–Colin Powell

In 1955, Walt Disney Production opened Disneyland in Anaheim, California. In 1959, after four successful years of Disneyland, Walt Disney Production started planning a second resort as a large version to address some of the lessons learned from Disneyland. In 1963, a site near Orlando, Florida, was selected for Walt Disney World Resort, and the initial phase resort opened in 1971 with one theme park and two hotels. Disney had a master plan for the site, including additional theme parks and a new city.

Using feedback from customers, Disney started to work on opening new theme parks in 1982, 1989, and 1998, water parks, golf courses, and hotels. Disney also built and closed venues that did not deliver value, such as the Walt Disney World Speedway. Within the theme parks, Disney regularly updates the attractions and facilities with a focus on their guests and making their visit as enjoyable as possible. From one theme park and two hotels, Walt Disney World Resort has grown to four theme parks, two water parks, four golf courses, and twenty-eight hotels!

The use of agile or iterative approaches to develop products is often associated with technology products. In fact, these approaches can be applied to all industries. Disney started with an MVP in Disneyland, learned from it, and created the Walt Disney World Resort opening with one theme park and two hotels. Over the years, Disney added attractions based on feedback from customers, responding to competition, and changes in technology.

Product Owners: The Solution

In Chapter 1, we shared the story of Kodak, the inventor and patent holder of the digital camera. Unfortunately, Kodak was not able to adopt the product and grow it to produce value for the customer and the organization. Instead, Kodak killed the idea based on existing market conditions and making false assumptions about the future. Within 25 years of inventing the digital camera, Kodak had filed for Chapter 11 bankruptcy protection. Kodak is not alone. There are many organizations that have developed products that have failed to grow and mature, and which made other organizations successful. There is a saying 'someone's failure is someone else's success,' these organizations show that having the right ingredients is what matters in business prosperity. The new generation of product owners is one of the main ingredients to help organizations develop products that deliver value to customers continuously, ensuring growth and sustainability.

Organizations face five challenges when it comes to strategy delivery: culture, structure, focus, execution, and change. The role of a new generation of product owners is to help organizations overcome these challenges. Product owners need to create and enforce a transparent environment, set priorities for the organization, make educated and fast decisions about the products they build. These products add value, react quickly to evolving conditions, empower customers, and synthesize feedback from a multitude of sources.

The new generation of product owners needs to acquire the skills to help organizations address the impacts of diversity, technology, and business models. These impacts are creating the challenges organizations and their products face every day. Throughout the book we have outlined the skills that are required by the new generation of product owners using the acronym **ACHIEVE**, standing for agility for business, crash the challenge, hone the team, iterate to make it happen, enable effective ownership, value sustained delivery, and excel as product owners.

Figure 8.1: ACHIEVE Product Ownership

As a new generation of product owners, you must go back to basics; to think about how to quickly deliver value to customers, simplify processes, build a great team, and continuously improve, as your organization changes. This has to be done while the environment around you is in a constant state of change. You have to listen to your customers by using the 3 R's: relate, reflect, and reshape to grasp meaningful feedback. You have to use the principles of lean to reduce

waste as you deliver great products to your customers. At the same time, you need to simplify everything allowing you to have the singular focus on delivering products so that you can satisfy your customers.

Product owners need to crash the challenges that organizations face. As the new generation of product owners, you must take ownership of your product. While organizations are giving you ownership of the products they produce, the new generation of product owners needs to delegate to their team members, to set the pattern for nurture and empowerment feelings toward the product. Not only that, product owners need to support the organization, but they need to support the team and changes required to deliver products. Product owners need to embrace the cultural change to improve productivity within the organization while understanding how benefits are being identified to match customer experience and acquisition measurements.

Product owners are leaders who need to know how to create **SMART** teams. Teams that have shared objectives, require minimal supervision, are accountable, respectful, and trustworthy. Product owners need to be able to use appropriate situational leadership styles to deal with supporting and growing the team. The new generation of product owners needs to create a team culture that fits within the organization culture and delivers the five principles of product culture (customer-driven mission, outcome over output or processes, leadership over management, team over function or tasks, and technology as a core asset) and four principles of value delivery (efficiency, collaboration, value, and flow).

The new generation of product owners needs to iterate to deliver value to customers through products. Start small and add features to the product based on the feedback received. Get the product in the hands of customers to experience it and build lovely memories. Product owners maintain the product backlog and always ensure that the team is constantly and consistently working on the highest priority features that give the greatest value to the customers while taking an agile approach in product delivery by deploying smaller packages of

features more frequently. This way a product can be completely transformed over time, simply by focusing on maximum value for each delivery. The user stories have associated acceptance criteria that ensure focused delivery of value to the customer and constant communications to elicit customer feedback. Product owners deliver the minimum viable product for the smallest valuable feature set and then continuously improve.

Product owners are first and foremost owners. The new generation of product owners do not visit, borrow, or rent products. Product owners take pride in ownership and delivery of the best product possible. Owning the product is attaching yourself to the product and believing in its capabilities to generate tangible benefits. Ownership is about caring for the object owned, taking it to the next level of growth and development. To develop great products, the product owner must work in close collaboration with other teams as they build the features that are required in the product and define the expected benefits. Working with the team and building a circle of trust between members of the team, other departments, and customers is what the new generation of product owners should do to break the silos and build success. Stakeholders and product owners are in a relationship of trust, representing the best interest of customers and delivering the maximum value.

The longevity of product life cycles and the value delivery streams are what makes product owners succeed in their roles. With the use of value stream mapping, product owners will ensure that value and quality are being delivered at every stage in the product life cycle. Further to that, measurement and feedback must be constantly monitored to continuously enhance a product to create additional value. Through iterations and continuous improvement, organizations will be better positioned to build and deliver products that speak value to customers over time.

Last, but not least, product owners must invest in continuous personal growth. They must learn new skills and capabilities to become

better product champions for their organizations and, most importantly for the customers that expect high-quality outcomes.

You are Worth It

Product owners are important assets for organizations to address the five challenges outlined in Chapter 1 and explored further in Chapters 2 through 7. These challenges have been presented time and time again by organizations, and a consolidated approach focused around the product can be the solution to every leader's concern.

Investment News interviewed executives from different organizations and found that the second cause for losing sleep at night for these leaders is fear of the competition. Jay Laschinger, SVP of Alliant Retirement Consulting confesses that his major fear is "Staying ahead of our competition." A competitor comes in and is talking about something you haven't brought up for whatever reason with your client, and then you are fighting to regain that confidence. You want to make sure you're delivering that value and not just get complacent" (Zhu, 2019).

A strategic approach around products must become the key to unlocking productivity improvement and increased value in organizations. Building product organizations and seeing sustainable customer value is a key element for long term strategy execution.

The first challenge is culture. The organization culture defines how things are done. As a product owner, you are in a unique position to focus on the five principles of product culture (customer-driven mission, outcome over output or processes, leadership over management, team over function or task, and technology as a core enabler). These principles in combination with the four principles of value delivery (efficiency, collaboration, value, flow), will prepare any organization for marketplace volatility and change. Culture is dictated by everyone's beliefs, behaviors, principles, and values; therefore, it is very important to foster an environment of constant growth and healthy competition inside teams and organizations overall. Many

companies develop a culture of entrepreneurship where employees are compensated in shares and see the impact on these shares first-hand. WestJet introduced this model as they wanted to have the employees directly affected or compensated by the way they would perform in the organization, taking ownership of their work to produce results and, contribute to market share increase.

The second challenge is structure. Some organizations have an organizational structure that makes it very difficult for people to perform. The organizational structure contains many barriers that prevent or slows down communications, creates roadblocks, or delay. Flatter organizations delegate product ownership to the product owner, then the product owner has the authority to manage a product through the life cycle. The product owner can focus on delivering value by having products that are profitable, that address customer concerns and build a good reputation in the marketplace.

At Valve, one of the most successful gaming companies, they have adopted a culture without structure. Staff is hired by the team based on the needs and employees are self-organized from the moment they start with the organization. In fact, the team welcomes the person on the first day, after which they must find meaningful work in the products they see value in. That is why the meaningful products that deliver value attract people and form self-managed flat teams. The organization chart at Valve looks like a cluster of always connected dots, always relying on each other in every direction.

The third challenge is focus. Many organizations are unable to deliver their strategic plan because they lose focus, or they have the wrong focus such as what features their competitor is offering or small changes inside the environment. A way to maintain focus on the product is to ensure the product will deliver the right amount of value to the customer. Focus should also be maintained at different levels of customer quadrant: satisfaction, experience, competition, and compliance. Feedback is fundamental for maintaining focus on all of these categories to build product sustainability from there.

The fourth challenge is execution. Organizations struggle to implement new products and services because their plans are too long-term focused, or they simply lack execution skills. The one-step is to build a strong execution framework with products focused on the value they deliver. To do this, product owners should obtain feedback from a variety of sources, especially customers, and ensure the feedback is added to the product backlog. The product owner should regularly review the product backlog and selected features that add the most value to customers. These features and grouped into product iterations that can be developed by teams. Once the enhanced product is launched, the cycle is repeated with the gathering of feedback from customers. Achievement of strategic objectives relies on the right products being developed and obtaining benefits from the products.

The last challenge is change. For organizations to be sustainable, their strategy must be flexible enough to adapt to changing priorities. In today's world, with increased diversity, disruptive technology, and new business models being introduced continuously, an organization needs to be aware of these impacts to current strategy and be willing to modify it as required. By keeping their strategy current, organizations will ensure they are meeting the needs of their customers in the long-term.

Figure 8.2: Challenges of Strategy Delivery

As a new generation of product owners, you must, own your product to support your organization in overcoming these five challenges of delivering strategy.

The Secret Sauce: Five Tips

It is all about you. If you want to be a new generation of product owners, the ones who care about their customers, then you are halfway there. Remember that, like in everything else, mindset is the major component for success. From there, you need to continue to improve your skills and capabilities to serve the purpose of your role and grow your career. The new generation of product owners must use these five skills:

- **Active Listening**. Developing your listening skills comes with practice. You need to find ways of listening to the customer to understand the real meaning of their feedback. The use of technology can help product owners get better at listening, collecting and analyzing feedback. By creating instant feedback venues such as chat or feedback prompts, product owners will get faster and situational feedback they can translate into decisions and actionable improvement plans. Customers absolutely value new features going to their product, but customers appreciate more knowing that they were heard and incorporating their feedback into the product. Addressing customer feedback will give much more loyalty to the organization than just delivering an enhanced product. Timing has become essential, more than ever, product owners need to know when and how customers buy the product, where the product is being purchased and how customer buying behavior is changing over time.

- **Driving value**. Everyone wants something, either an expensive car, a bigger house or a luxury vacation home. Do we actually need all these? The new generation of product owners must be able to differentiate between wants and needs. Product owners set priorities based on the 'must-haves', not

on 'wish lists'. By delivering the needs, meaning the necessities, is a way to add more value to customers. The wants, meaning the desires, can be later implemented and, most of the time, end up in the waste bucket for they have no practical use. It is also known that 'needs' build customer satisfaction, whereas 'wants' are only temporary incentives.

- **Focusing**. Product owners should constantly review their products and look for that one feature that shines in the product. It is a unique feature that makes your product shine in front of customers, and that delivers the maximum value to them. This feature has some characteristics. First, it is unique, and it creates an experience that no product can offer. Second, it gives customers the ultimate value, something that they cannot leave without. When Steve Jobs decided to include the mouse with the Macintosh PC, it became a star feature. The mouse allowed users to interface in a new and exciting way, without having to use the keyboard.

- **Promoting**. Product owners spend a huge amount of time marketing their products. They need to understand the sales and marketing functions of their organization as often these two departments are the most common pipeline for product owners. A product without a marketing strategy is like a flower without water. It will have a limited survival period and will die suddenly, being replaced by something else. Many times, ideas die because of a lack of marketing plans and investment. Lack of promotion is lack of execution. Launched in 2009, the Nook was a new version of the tablet produced by Barnes & Noble. The sales picked up at some point and then plunged rapidly making the product extinct in a matter of months. Brian Sozzi, the chief equities strategist at Belus Capital Advisors, provided an explanation: *"Shoppers couldn't get beyond Barnes & Noble being a destination for something they no longer want or generally care about, books. Barnes & Noble management perpetuated that by not*

investing aggressively enough in marketing to alter perception." (Lutz, 2014)

- **Learning**. Product owners should continue to focus on gaining additional skills as they begin or continue their development journey. Constantly gather valuable feedback to synthesize into learning. Learning has become a necessity in today's workplace given the amount of information that is exchanged continuously and the changes in technology. Lessons learned or lunch and learn sessions should be tools often used by teams and leaders. Sharing learning experiences and discussing opportunities for skill development should be a common practice in high-performing teams. Being aware of the available tools and skills needed for product development, as well as customer interactions is what will keep the new generation of product owners competitive and engaged in their practice. It is all about the need to keep a sharp mind. In his book, *The 7 Habits of Highly Successful People*, Steven Covey identifies the seventh habit as being 'Sharpen the Saw' *(Covey, 2016)*. This habit is a reminder to invest the time in building the skills and knowledge to deal with situations at work because you will only be successful if you remain current in the work you do. Take the time necessary to invest in yourself and to refresh your mind as often as possible.

These five tips are beneficial for the new generation of product owners to build credibility with all product stakeholders and maximize the value products are producing. They can guide you as the product owner interacting with the team, with your customer, with the product you are developing. You are not alone, and you have a whole new generation of product owners joining you in the journey of creating success stories for your organization, your team and yourself.

Figure 8.3: Five Tips for Product Owners

Take Your Value to the Next Level

The role of the product owner is continuously evolving and changing in organizations from different industry sectors. It is hard to predict the future of such a role; however, current situations are favorable for the growth of this role over the next few years. The complexity of the role, the engagement with stakeholders and the budget account-ability make the role desirable by business analysts, project managers, project leaders, and application specialists. The world of role segregation is also seeing an interesting turn, where organizations have started to encourage cross-functioning roles and skill sharing, for people to take advantage of the surrounding acumen and transition easily in multiple roles if the strategic focus changes.

Here are some suggestions where product owners can focus on improving their expertise and thinking to be successful. The first is to start thinking about your organization as a product organization, with products aligned around a portfolio of products. Many organizations have started already, using an organizing model around lines of busi-

ness with identifiable value streams. A line of business can be a collection of products following the same overall theme, distinct features or customers, and diverse value generation points. Organizations should group products together into product portfolios and manage these portfolios in an effective way, aligned with the organization's strategy. Portfolios can include products at different stages in their product life cycle, whether it is in the launching, development, maturity or retirement stages. This is a way for organizations to balance risk in product development and encourage creativity and innovation. Portfolios are driven by profit and are created around value streams. Based on the value they produce through their products, they can get funding for their initiatives to produce more value.

Business lines are always striving to create more value so they can obtain more funding for new initiatives that will produce added value and encourage growth. Product portfolios are not new; some organizations have had them for many years. It is even more important in today's age, as organizations are struggling with the challenges discussed in Chapter 1 that they think about having product portfolios to help diversify their risk, help provide more flexibility and strengthen alignment to strategy. The new generation of product owners needs to link their products to the right product portfolio and realize, within that portfolio, the value that contributes to the organization's success.

The second area a product owner can expand their skills is to understand the bigger picture of what is happening in today's marketplace. This book started talking about the challenges of diversity, technology, and business model. Product owners should understand the impacts of these trends on their organization. Picture yourself as a product owner in the taxi business. Did you think about the impact of technology and smartphones on your business? Were you thinking about how you could develop an app for a smartphone to allow your customers to order taxis to their house and to pay any way they wanted? Or were you trying to think about how to get the next car on the road and how to deal with customer complaints? Most taxi

companies were thinking about just running their business efficiently. It was not until Garrett Camp and Travis Kalanick co-founders of Uber came up with a better solution to match riders and drivers using a smartphone app that the taxi industry had a wake-up call. By then, it was too late for the taxi business. Product owners need to look around and absorb what is happening in the world, how that could impact their products, and what can be done to stay competitive and innovative at all times. To do this, product owners need to be curious. They need to ask questions and have an open mind to think about future possibilities and not just limit themselves to current ones. Be revolutionary, stay ahead and stay fresh.

Today, there are significant changes all happening at an unprecedented rate. There is less and less certainty and predictability in this world, and this is causing problems for organizations. Product strategies and the organizations they serve are failing at alarming rates. In 1965, the average tenure of companies on the S&P 500 was 33 years. By 1990, it was 20 years. It is forecasted to shrink to 14 years by 2026 *(Mochari, 2016)*. To address the challenges they will face, organizations need the new generation of product owners who care about customers, value, and sustainability.

Are you ready to join the new generation of product owners?

Glossary

3Rs: three customer sides of listening to customers: relate, reflect, and reshape.

4Ps: a term used to describe the four elements of marketing: price, promotion, place, and product.

5Ps: a term used to describe the five characteristics of product ownership: pride, power, promotion, protection, and passion.

5-Star method: uses a five-point scale to obtain immediate feedback on the product. Often used immediately after the use of an online product or service.

Backlog: A list of features that are selected in a priority order to add to a product to deliver the most value to customers. As known as the product backlog.

Blue Ocean: an approach to develop an organization's strategy developed by W. Chan Kim and Renee Mauborgne.

Bloomberg's bullpen: a large open office of 50 work statements created by Michael Bloomberg when he was mayor of New York to help foster openness and communication in the city government.

Butterfly effect: from Chaos theory, where a small change in one state can cause large differences in a later state.

Brightline: A division of the Project Management Institute focused on strategy implementation, see www.brightline.com.

C-Level: refers to senior management with the titles of Chief Executive Officer (CEO), Chief Operating Officer (COO), Chief Marketing Officer (CMO), Chief Information Officer (CIO), etc.

CHAOS Report: a report created annually by The Standish Group on the success of the IT project.

Clan: is a type of culture that is like an extended family unit, as used in the Spotify structure example.

Cross-functional team: a group of people working together that have a variety of skills and capabilities.

Consumerism: Is the protection or promotion of customer interests.

Customer: the person buying or using the product. Also called a consumer or user.

Cycle time: The total time from the beginning to the end of your process, as defined by you and your customer.

Epic: A large body of work that can be broken down into several smaller stories.

Feature: functionality or capability to be added to a product.

Fintech: Financial technology is a technology that provides banking services using digital and online technologies.

Flat organization: an organizational structure with minimal levels of management and each manager having many direct reports.

Lead time: The time between the initiation and completion of a production process.

Lean: an approach to systematically minimizing waste without sacrificing productivity and adding value; initially developed as the Toyota Production System.

Kanban: a tool that can be used to track the progress of complete tasks.

Mysterious shopper method: a researcher assumes the role of a customer to get the same experience as a customer is a particular situation.

Organization: the group that uses people and resources to create products which include: companies, corporations, non-profits, charities, non-governmental organizations, governments, etc.

Playing to Win: an approach to develop an organization's strategy developed by A.G. Lafley and Roger L. Martin.

Porter's Five Forces: an approach to analyzing the environment in which an organization operates developed by Michael Porter. The five forces are Competition in the industry; Potential of new entrants

into the industry; Power of suppliers; Power of customers, and Threat of substitute products.

Portfolio: A portfolio is a collection of products or services offered by an organization.

Product: a product or service that an organization provides to customers or uses internally to operate the organization.

Product Owner: the person who has responsibility and accountability for a product. Also called a Product Manager.

Project-based: is an organization structure consisting of multi-functional teams focused on delivering projects.

Roadmap: provides a plan of when features are planned to be delivered over time.

Scenario Thinking: an approach to develop an organization's strategy based on systems thinking.

Scientific management: a management theory that analyzes workflows to improve efficiency and labor productivity invented by Fredrick Taylor in the late 1800s.

Scrum: is a framework to address complex problems, often used to develop software, www.scrum.org.

Sectors: a division of the economy into a group of organizations doing similar work, for example, information technology, energy, health care, etc.

Self-managing team: a group of people working together with no assigned leader or manager. It is expected that the team will organize their work.

Service Level Agreement (SLA): Is a contract between a service provider and a customer defining the standards of service to be provided.

Story: a description of part of a feature that delivers value to customers, which are also called a user story. It can be written in the following structured approach, as an <Who> I need to <What> so that <Why>.

Takt time: The average time between the start of production of one unit and the start of production of the next unit when these production starts are set to match the rate of customer demand.

Team: A team is a group of people working together for a common goal or result. It can include project teams, product teams, delivery teams, marketing teams, development teams, etc.

Uptimes: The time during which a machine or device is in operation.

Value stream: A set of steps from the start of value creation to the delivery of a product to customers.

Waste: An act or instance of using or expending something carelessly, extravagantly, or to no purpose.

References

Chapter 1

Agile Alliance. "What Is a Minimum Viable Product (MVP)?" *Agile Alliance*, 25 Sept. 2019, www.agilealliance.org/glossary/mvp/#q=~(infinite~false~filters~(tags~(~'mvp))~searchTerm~'~sort~false~sortDirection~'asc~page~1).

Bulygo, Zach. "Tony Hsieh, Zappos, and the Art of Great Company Culture." *Neil Patel*, 15 Feb. 2019, neilpatel.com/blog/zappos-art-of-culture/.

Castellion, George, and Stephen K. Markham. "Myths About New Product Failure Rates." *New Product Success*, 5 Sept. 2018, newproductsuccess.org/new-product-failure-rates-2013-jpim-30-pp-976-979/.

Emmer, Marc. "95 Percent of New Products Fail. Here Are 6 Steps to Make Sure Yours Don't." *Inc.com, Inc.*, 6 July 2018, www.inc.com/marc-emmer/95-percent-of-new-products-fail-here-are-6-steps-to-make-sure-yours-dont.html.

Estrin, James. "Kodak's First Digital Moment." *The New York Times*, The New York Times, 12 Aug. 2015, lens.blogs.nytimes.com/2015/08/12/kodaks-first-digital-moment/.

Goldin, Ian, and Chris Kutarna. *Age of Discovery: Navigating the Storms of Our Second Renaissance*. Bloomsbury Information, 2016.

Hanlon, Annmarie. "How to Use the BCG Matrix - Smart Insights Digital Marketing." *Smart Insights*, 16 July 2019, www.smartinsights.com/marketing-planning/marketing-models/use-bcg-matrix/.

Howard, Eric, and Myint Htay. "The Evolution of the Industrial Ages: Industry 1.0 to 4.0." *Success in Simulation and Scheduling*, 5 Sept. 2018, www.simio.com/blog/2018/09/05/evolution-industrial-ages-industry-1-0-4-0/.

Neilson, Gary L., et al. "The Secrets to Successful Strategy Execution." *Harvard Business Review*, 16 July 2015, hbr.org/2008/06/the-secrets-to-successful-strategy-execution.

RankingTheWorld. "Top 10 Most Valuable Companies In The World (1997-2019)." *YouTube*, YouTube, 28 Apr. 2019, www.youtube.com/watch?v=8WVoJ6JNLO8.

Tokareva, Julia. "What Is A Minimum Viable Product, And Why Do Companies Need Them?" *Forbes*, Forbes Magazine, 27 Feb. 2018, www.forbes.com/sites/quora/2018/02/27/what-is-a-minimum-viable-product-and-why-do-companies-need-them/#464c7ec6382c.

"VUCA World - LEADERSHIP SKILLS & STRATEGIES." *VUCA*, 2019, www.vuca-world.org/.

Chapter 2

Dames, Karin. "What Does an Agile Mind Look like?" Medium, Medium, 9 Aug. 2016, medium.com/@funficient/what-does-an-agile-mind-look-like-12f21cb3a20.

McChrystal, Stanley A., et al. *Team of Teams: New Rules of Engagement for a Complex World*. Portfolio/Penguin, 2015.

Pichler, Hannes, et al. "Less Can Be More for Product Portfolios." Https://Www.bcg.com, 25 Aug. 2014, www.bcg.com/en-ca/publications/2014/lean-manufacturing-consumers-products-less-can-be-more-for-product-portfolio-attacking-complexity-while-enhancing-the-value-of-diversity.aspx.

Staples, Sandra. "Agile / Lean Development - Waste Is Eliminated."
     Medium, Ingeniously Simple, 27 July 2018,

The Standship Group, "The CHAOS Report (1994)." *The Standish
     Group*, The Standish Group International Inc, 1995,
     https://www.standishgroup.com/sample_re-
     search_files/chaos_report_1994.pdf.

Varhol, Peter. "The Complete History of Agile Software Develop-
     ment." *TechBeacon*, TechBeacon, 22 Jan. 2019, techbea-
     con.com/app-dev-testing/agility-beyond-history-legacy-ag-
     ile-development.

Chapter 3

Denning, Stephanie. "The Netflix Pressure-Cooker: A Culture That
     Drives Performance." *Forbes*, Forbes Magazine, 26 Oct.
     2018, www.forbes.com/sites/stephanieden-
     ning/2018/10/26/the-netflix-pressure-cooker-a-culture-
     that-drives-performance/#27b41c39151a.

Hsieh, Tony. *Delivering Happiness: A Path to Profits, Passion, and
     Purpose*. Grand Central Pub., 2013.

Killelea, Grace. *The Confidence Effect: Every Women's Guide to the
     Attitude That Attracts Success*. AMACOM, 2016.

Leadership Forces, "The Art of Delegation: How to Win with a Dele-
     gating Leadership Style." *Leadership Forces*, 23 June 2019,
     www.leadershipforces.com/art-delegation/.

Narus, James C. Anderson, James A. "Business Marketing: Under-
     stand What Customers Value*." Harvard Business Review*, 1
     Aug. 2014, hbr.org/1998/11/business-marketing-under-
     stand-what-customers-value.

Taguiam, Sarah, and Sara Mojtehedzadeh. "Workplace Happiness? There's an App for That." *Thestar.com*, 11 Nov. 2014, www.thestar.com/business/2014/11/11/workplace_happiness_theres_an_app_for_that.html.

Webb, Maynard. "Five Steps To Delegating More Effectively." *Forbes*, Forbes Magazine, 21 Aug. 2017, www.forbes.com/sites/maynardwebb/2017/08/21/five-steps-to-help-you-delegate-more-effectively/#7ff2753d47ed.

Zappos Insights, "The Zappos Triangle of Accountability." *Zappos Insights*, 2019, www.zapposinsights.com/triangle-of-accountability.

Chapter 4

Denning, Stephanie. "The Netflix Pressure-Cooker: A Culture That Drives Performance." *Forbes*, Forbes Magazine, 26 Oct. 2018, www.forbes.com/sites/stephaniedenning/2018/10/26/the-netflix-pressure-cooker-a-culture-that-drives-performance/#27b41c39151a.

Folz, Christina. "10 Tips for Changing Your Company's Culture-and Making It Stick." *SHRM*, SHRM, 16 Aug. 2019, www.shrm.org/resourcesandtools/hr-topics/employee-relations/pages/10-tips-for-changing-your-companys-culture%E2%80%94and-making-it-stick.aspx.

Garton, Michael Mankins, Eric, et al. "How Spotify Balances Employee Autonomy and Accountability." *Harvard Business Review*, 9 Feb. 2017, hbr.org/2017/02/how-spotify-balances-employee-autonomy-and-accountability.

Goetzmann, Jens-Fabian. "Google & Apple - A Tale of Two Product Cultures." *Medium*, The Startup, 14 May 2019, medium.com/swlh/google-apple-a-tale-of-two-product-cultures-e86c62823961.

Hiatt, Jeff. "ADKAR Change Management Model Overview." *Prosci*, 2003, www.prosci.com/adkar/adkar-model.

Inniss, Dianne. "Change Management in the Agile World - Willing, Able and Ready." *ThoughtWorks*, 15 May 2019, www.thoughtworks.com/insights/blog/change-management-agile-world-getting-ready-war.

Kaur, Khushpreet. "How to Go Agile Enterprise-Wide: An Interview with Scott Richardson." *McKinsey & Company*, Aug. 2017, www.mckinsey.com/business-functions/mckinsey-digital/our-insights/how-to-go-agile-enterprise-wide-an-interview-with-scott-richardson.

Keller, Scott, and Mary Meaney. "High-Performing Teams: A Timeless Leadership Topic." *McKinsey & Company*, June 2017, www.mckinsey.com/business-functions/organization/our-insights/high-performing-teams-a-timeless-leadership-topic.

Lencioni, Patrick. *The Five Dysfunctions of a Team*. Jossey-Bass, 2012.

Lindwall, Kristian. "How Music Streaming Giant Spotify Stays Successful." *Planet Lean*, 6 Nov. 2018, planet-lean.com/spotify-agile-leadership-lean/.

Little, Jason. "Navigating Organizational Change*." Lean Change Management*, 16 Feb. 2014, leanchange.org/2014/02/navigating-organizational-change/.

McChrystal, Stanley A., et al. *Team of Teams: New Rules of Engagement for a Complex World*. Portfolio/Penguin, 2015.

Weil, Elizabeth. "Every Leader Tells a Story." *Fast Company*, Fast Company, 30 July 2012, www.fastcompany.com/34330/every-leader-tells-story.

Chapter 5

Anthony, Scott D. "Innovation and Iteration: Friends Not Foes." *Harvard Business Review*, 23 July 2014, hbr.org/2008/05/innovation-and-iteration-frien.

Blank, Steve. "Why the Lean Start-Up Changes Everything." *Harvard Business Review*, May 2013, hbr.org/2013/05/why-the-lean-start-up-changes-everything.

Patton, Jeff, et al. *User Story Mapping*. O'Reilly, 2014.

Ries, Eric. *The Lean Startup: How Today's Entrepreneurs Use Continuous Innovation to Create Radically Successful Business*. Crown Business, 2011.

Rogers, Philip. "Back to Basics: Writing and Splitting User Stories." *Medium*, Innovative Agile Techniques and Practices, 7 Jan. 2018, medium.com/agile-outside-the-box/back-to-basics-writing-and-splitting-user-stories-8903a931499c.

Roos, Dave. "10 Companies That Completely Reinvented Themselves." *HowStuffWorks*, HowStuffWorks, 10 Jan. 2014, money.howstuffworks.com/10-companies-reinvented-themselves.htm.

Upbin, Bruce. "Silicon Valley Isn't Innovative, It's Iterative: Four Proof Points." *Forbes*, Forbes Magazine, 9 Apr. 2014, www.forbes.com/sites/ciocentral/2014/04/08/silicon-valley-isnt-innovative-its-iterative-four-proof-points/.

Yoxall, James. "MVPs Can Be Dangerous." *IndigoBlue*, 2016, www.indigoblue.co.uk/blog-posts/mvps-can-be-dangerous-minimum-viable-product-agile.

Chapter 6

Gasca, Peter. "4 Steps to Building a Great Product-Focused Organization." *Entrepreneur*, 17 Aug. 2015, www.entrepreneur.com/article/249580.

Reina, Dennis, and Michelle Reina. *Trust and Betrayal in the Workplace: Building Effective Relationships in Your Organization.* Berrett-Koehler Publishers, Inc., 2015.

Chapter 7

Allred, Jesse, and Mike Wilson. "Kaizen Case Study: Siemens Oostkamp." *Kaizen News*, 16 Oct. 2019, www.kaizen-news.com/kaizen-case-study-siemens-oostkamp/.

Golub, Harvey, et al. "Delivering Value to Customers." *McKinsey & Company*, June 2000, www.mckinsey.com/business-functions/strategy-and-corporate-finance/our-insights/delivering-value-to-customers.

Kaufman, Josh. *The Personal MBA: A World-Class Business Education in a Single Volume.* Portfolio, 2012.

Lee, Yen Nee. "Fintech Start-Ups Are Now More Ready to Work with Banks, Says ANZ Exec." *CNBC*, CNBC, 28 June 2019, www.cnbc.com/2019/06/27/fintech-start-ups-are-now-more-ready-to-work-with-banks-says-anz-coo.html.

Martin, Karen, and Mike Osterling. *Value Stream Mapping: How to Visualize Work and Align Leadership for Organizational Transformation.* McGraw-Hill, 2014.

Chapter 8

Covey, Stephen R. *The 7 Habits of Highly Effective People.* Franklin-Covey Co., 2016.

Lutz, Ashley. "4 Reasons Barnes & Noble's Nook Crashed And Burned." *Business Insider*, Business Insider, 9 Jan. 2014, www.businessinsider.com/reasons-barnes-and-noble-nook-is-failing-2014-1.

Mochari, Ilan. "Why Half of the S&P 500 Companies Will Be Replaced in the Next Decade." *Inc.com, Inc.*, 23 Mar. 2016, www.inc.com/ilan-mochari/innosight-sp-500-new-companies.html.

Zhu, Ellie. "What Keeps These Executives up at Night?" *InvestmentNews*, 18 May 2019, www.investmentnews.com/article/20190518/FREE/190519940/what-keeps-these-executives-up-at-night.

Index

Made in the USA
Middletown, DE
17 November 2019

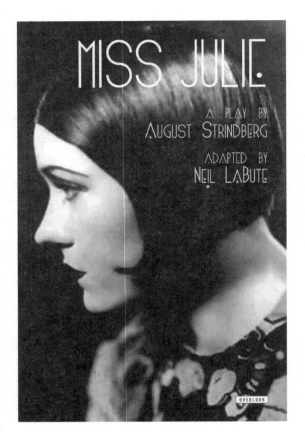

In this powerful adaption, Neil LaBute embraces the glittering darkness of *Woyzeck's* violent, erotic, inhumane world and uncompromisingly makes it his own. From his opening in an operating theatre and then scene by macabre scene, LaBute imbues this classic with his singular intensity and moral vision, as he takes it to its nightmarish conclusion.

Included in this volume is Neil LaBute's provocative new monologue "Kandahar," in which a soldier back from Afghanistan calmly explains his devastating actions of the day before. A gripping stand-alone piece, this short work is also a trenchant modern-day exploration of the potent and enduring themes of *Woyzeck*.

$14.95   978-1-4683-101-9

With little to occupy their time other than finding a decent place to hang out—the zoo, the mall, the school parking lot—Darrell and Tim are two American teenagers who lack any direction or purpose in their lives. When Darrell's suspicion about the faithlessness of his girlfriend is confirmed and Tim comes to her defense, there is nothing to brake their momentum as all three speed toward disaster.

"LaBute . . . gets inside the emptiness of American culture, the masquerade and the evil of neglect. *The Distance from Here*, it seems to me, is a new title to be added to the short list of important contemporary plays."   —**John Lahr**, *The New Yorker*

$14.95   978-1-58567-371-1

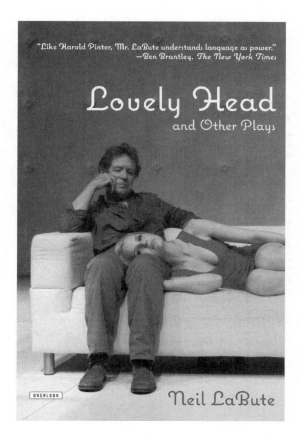

The title play, which had its American premiere at La MaMa in 2012, rivetingly explores the relationship between a nervous older man and a glib young prostitute, as their evening together drives toward a startling conclusion.

Also included is the one-act play *The Great War*, which looks at a divorcing couple and the ground they need to cross to reach their own end of hostilities; *In the Beginning*, which was written as a response to the Occupy movement and produced around the world in 2012-13 as part of *Theatre Uncut*; *The Wager*, the stage version of the film *Double or Nothing* starring Adam Brody; the two-handers *A Guy Walks Into a Bar, Over the River and Through the Woods,* and *Strange Fruit;* and two powerful new monologues, *Bad Girl* and *The Pony of Love.*

$16.95   978-1-4683-0705-4